The Bungalow Mystery

The man chained to the bench was Jacob Aborn!

NANCY DREW MYSTERY STORIES

The Bungalow Mystery

BY CAROLYN KEENE

PUBLISHERS *Grosset & Dunlap* NEW YORK

A NATIONAL GENERAL COMPANY

Contents

The Bungalow Mystery

CHAPTER I

A Blinding Storm

"Look at those black storm clouds!" Nancy Drew pointed out to her friend, Helen Corning, who was seated beside her in the bow of the small red motorboat.

Nancy, blue-eyed, and with reddish-gold glints in her blond hair, was at the wheel. She gazed anxiously across a long expanse of water to the distant shores of Twin Lakes. The Pinecrest Motel, where the eighteen-year-old girl and her older friend were staying, was almost two miles away on the smaller of the two lakes.

Helen Corning, dark-haired and petite, looked at Nancy with concern. "I think we're in for a cloudburst," she said, "and Twin Lakes becomes as rough as the ocean in a storm."

A few minutes later angry waves began to beat against the sides of the boat.

"Are there life preservers aboard, Helen?" Nancy asked.

"No," Helen answered fearfully.

Nancy set her chin grimly. Although it was only four o'clock in the afternoon, the sky was becoming increasingly dark. The pleasant summer breeze, which had been blowing earlier, was turning into a stiff wind.

"It's getting harder to keep on course," Nancy remarked, gripping the wheel more tightly.

As she increased the boat's speed to the maximum, the craft fairly leaped through the water, dashing spray into the girls' faces.

"I wonder if there are any raincoats in the lockers," said Helen.

"Please look," Nancy requested. "We'll be drenched by the time we reach the motel dock."

Luckily Helen found two plastic coats. She slipped into one, then helped Nancy into the other.

A streak of forked lightning cut across the sky, momentarily disclosing a thick mass of ugly clouds. The lightning was followed by an ominous crack of thunder, which caused the girls to jump.

"This is terrible!" Helen wailed.

A moment later the wind began to howl. It struck the boat with a force which made Helen grasp the railing next to her for support. Another dazzling flash of lightning illuminated the sky, and simultaneously a deluge of rain began to descend.

Nancy peered ahead into the dimness. The shore line had vanished and the blinding rain made it impossible for her to see more than a few feet beyond the bow of the boat.

"At least we have half a tank of fuel," Nancy announced, trying to sound optimistic. "We'll reach shore soon, I'm sure."

"I wouldn't bet on that," Helen said nervously.

A worried expression furrowed the young pilot's brow. The boat was making little progress against the wind. If anything happened to the motor they would be at the mercy of the waves.

A few minutes later the rain came down even harder. The wind continued to blow a raging gale and the waves seemed higher.

The girls leaned forward, trying to get their bearings. As a jagged ribbon of lightning illuminated the path ahead, Helen screamed, "About!"

Nancy froze with horror. A tremendous log was floating directly into the path of the motorboat!

Her heart pounding, the young skipper gave the wheel a vicious turn, but not quickly enough. With a splintering crash, the bow of the boat struck the log!

The impact sent Helen sprawling to the deck. Nancy clung to the steering wheel, but was thrown forward violently.

"Helen, are you hurt?" she asked.

"I— I'm all right. Are you?" she stammered, as Nancy helped Helen to her feet. Both girls were breathing heavily.

By now the small boat was listing sharply to starboard. Nancy saw instantly that the log had torn a jagged hole in the side of the craft. Water was pouring in rapidly.

"Quick, Helen!" Nancy ordered tersely. "You bail and I'll try to stop the leak!"

She sprang forward, tore off her raincoat, and stuffed it into the hole. Helen, meanwhile, found a rusty can and began to bail. Despite their efforts, water continued to pour through the opening.

"Let's shout for help!" Nancy cried above the
wind, but she doubted that there was any other
craft on the lake.

The girls cupped their hands to their lips and shouted frantically. Their only answer was the howl of the gale and the steady beat of rain.

"Louder!" Helen urged, and they screamed until they were hoarse.

"It's no use," Nancy said at last. "We'll have to think of something else."

Just then Nancy saw a giant wave bearing down on them. She met it head on, hoping to ride the crest, but a deluge of water almost inundated the girls. They were flung overboard and the motor-boat sank to the bottom of the lake!

An excellent swimmer, Nancy managed to get her head above water almost immediately. Her first thought was for Helen. What had become of her?

Treading water, Nancy glanced about. Helen was not in sight.

"I must find her!" Nancy thought desperately. "She may have been injured!"

Then, several yards away, Nancy saw a white hand flash above the water. With powerful crawl strokes she plowed through the waves to the spot. The hand had vanished!

Nancy made a neat surface dive. Opening her eyes, she tried to see through the clouded water but to no avail. At last, she surfaced and drew in a deep breath.

Clearing her eyes, Nancy was relieved to spot her friend several feet ahead. Helen was floating on her back. Strong strokes brought Nancy directly behind her friend.

"My arms feel numb," Helen said weakly. "Guess I hit them on the boat."

"Don't worry," said Nancy. "Just lie still and I'll tow you to shore."

Nancy, however, had grave misgivings regarding her ability to accomplish this in the turbulent water. She needed every ounce of strength to swim the distance alone. *Could* she manage to save Helen? The storm had made the water very cold. Nancy prayed that she would not get a cramp and both girls go down.

"Hold your breath when you see a wave coming," she instructed Helen, as they started off.

At frequent intervals Nancy shouted for help, although she felt it was wasted energy. On and on they went.

Helen noticed finally that Nancy's breathing showed the great strain on her. "Save yourself," she begged. "Go on to shore without me."

"Never!" said Nancy, as a huge wave bore down upon the two girls, smothering them in its impact.

Feebly, Nancy struggled back to the surface with her burden. "One more like that and I'll be through," she said to herself.

Just then Nancy thought she detected a voice above the roar of the wind. Was it her imagination or had she really heard someone call?

"Help!" she screamed.

This time there could be no mistake, for she distinguished the words:

"Hold on! I'm coming!"

Through the blinding rain Nancy caught a glimpse of a dark object. A rowboat! If only she could hold out until it reached her!

"Over here!" Nancy cried loudly, waving.

As the boat approached, she fully expected to see it swamped. The boat swept safely toward the two girls, barely avoiding a crash, however. To Nancy's surprise, there was only one occupant in the boat—a slender, auburn-haired girl of about sixteen.

Twice she tried to bring the boat alongside the swimmers, but failed. The third time, as the craft swept past, Nancy lunged forward and caught the side of it. She dragged Helen along, supporting her with one hand until she, too, secured a hold.

"Can you climb aboard?" their rescuer asked. "I'll balance the boat while you get in."

Nancy explained about the submerged motorboat and Helen's useless arms.

With the strange girl and Nancy working together, they managed to get Helen into the craft. Then Nancy pulled herself over the side.

"Safe!" Helen said in relief. "I don't know how to thank you," she told their rescuer.

"Are you both all right?" asked the strange girl. "We're not far from the beach—otherwise, I couldn't have heard your cries for help in this wind."

"You were very brave to come for us," said Nancy. "I'm Nancy Drew and this is Helen Corning."

The girl at the oars stared at Nancy with keen interest. "I'm Laura Pendleton," she said. "I read in a newspaper about one of the mysteries you solved. I may need your help some day soon, Nancy."

Without another word Laura bent over her oars again.

"I'll help you row," Nancy offered, snatching up an extra oar from the bottom of the rowboat, and wondering what Laura Pendleton's mystery was.

Using the oar like a paddle, Nancy attempted to keep the boat on course. As she and Laura made some progress against the wind and waves, Helen took new hope.

"I think we're going to make it!" she said in relief. "Oh!"

A vivid flash of lightning illuminated the water. Directly ahead, through the rain, she and Nancy caught a glimpse of the rocky shore line.

"The rocks, Laura! Be careful or we'll be dashed against them!" Helen cried out, as the rowboat was tossed and slapped by the crashing waves.

Another zigzag streak of lightning disclosed the shore line more distinctly. A short distance out from the land and directly in front of their boat stood the ugly protruding nose of a jagged boulder!

CHAPTER II

Uninvited Guests

FOR an instant Nancy panicked. Would the girls be able to steer clear of the menacing rocks? A collision seemed unavoidable!

"We'll be killed!" gasped Helen.

"Row to the left, Laura!" Nancy commanded. "It's our only chance."

With a burst of energy the rowers turned the boat and deftly avoided the jagged boulder. An oncoming wave pushed them farther out of danger.

"There's a cove ahead!" Laura shouted above the wind. "We'll try to make it."

In another five minutes they reached the cove. Here the water was comparatively quiet.

"Thank goodness!" Helen murmured. "Oh, you girls are wonderful!"

As Nancy's oar struck a sand bar, she dropped it and quickly stepped out into water up to her knees. Laura followed and the two girls pulled the boat up onto the beach. Then they helped Helen Corning step onto firm sand.

"How do your arms feel now?" Nancy asked her.

"Better," Helen replied. "But I'm freezing." Her teeth were chattering.

Nancy herself was cold. She squinted through the darkness and rain, trying to see where they were. It seemed to be a desolate spot.

"Where are we?" she asked Laura. "Is there some place nearby where we can sit out the storm and get warm?"

"The only place I know," Laura replied, "is a bungalow I passed a while ago as I was walking along the beach. It's to our right, secluded among the trees."

"Sounds fine," Nancy said. "Let's hurry!"

The three bedraggled girls stumbled along the beach. Water oozed from Laura's sandals. Nancy and Helen had kicked theirs off in the lake and now slipped and slid in their soggy socks.

Presently the girls reached a small, concealed building, a one-and-a-half-storied weather-beaten bungalow which stood a short distance from the water's edge. The upper level nestled into the steep, wooded hillside. Since there was no light inside, Nancy assumed no one was there. She knocked. No answer. Nancy tried to open the door. It was locked.

"Looks as if we're out of luck," said Helen.

But Nancy was not easily discouraged, and she knew it was imperative for the girls to get warm. Her father, a well-known lawyer, had trained her to be self-reliant. He frequently handled mystery cases, and Nancy had often helped him in unearthing valuable clues.

In addition, Nancy had solved some mystery cases on her own—one involving an old clock and another a haunted house. There, Nancy had aided its owners to discover a hidden staircase which led to the capture of the mansion's "ghost."

"I'm sure that the owner of this bungalow will forgive us for going in," Nancy said.

There was a small window to the right of the door. She tried it and found to her relief that it was unlocked.

"That's a lucky break," said Helen, as Nancy opened the window.

Fortunately, it was low enough to the ground for the girls to hoist themselves through easily.

"Whew!" Laura exclaimed, as the wind almost blew them inside. She helped Nancy close the window.

It was pitch dark inside the building. Nancy groped around for a light switch, finally found one, and flicked it on. A small bulb in the ceiling disclosed nothing except two canoes and a wooden bench which stood against one wall.

"Maybe it's only a boathouse," said Helen, flopping wearily onto the bench.

The girls noticed a narrow flight of stairs leading to the second floor.

"I wonder," Nancy mused, "if we might find something up there to wrap around us. Or maybe even some towels to dry ourselves off with. Let's see."

Laura followed Nancy to the rear of the building. Seeing a light switch for the upper story, Nancy turned it and the two girls climbed the steps. To their surprise, the second floor of the bungalow was furnished with two cots and blankets, a table and chairs, tiny refrigerator, a sink, and a two-burner electric stove.

"We're in luck!" Nancy exclaimed happily. "Come on up, Helen," she called.

Laura spotted an open closet in a corner of the room. It was well stocked with food. She held up a can of prepared cocoa.

"Under the circumstances," she said, "I doubt that the owner of this place would object if we made something warm to drink."

Helen and Nancy agreed. Within a short time the three girls had taken off their wet clothing and were wrapped in blankets. Laura had turned on one burner of the stove and made hot chocolate.

"Umm, this is good," Nancy said contentedly.

Both she and Helen again thanked Laura profusely for coming to their rescue, and said they had been trying to get back to the Pinecrest Motel.

"Are you staying there?" Laura questioned.

"For a week," Helen replied. "My Aunt June is coming tomorrow. She was supposed to ride up with us Thursday from River Heights where we live, but was detained. She's going to help design my dress for my marriage to Jim Archer. He's in Europe now on business for an oil company. When he returns to the States, we'll be married."

Nancy Drew asked Laura if she, too, was a summer visitor at the resort. When her question met with silence, Nancy was surprised to see tears gathering in Laura's eyes.

"I'm sorry, Laura," Nancy said instantly. "You've been through a terrible ordeal. You should be resting instead of talking."

"Of course," Helen agreed.

Laura blinked her eyes, then said soberly, "You don't understand. You see, my mother passed away a month ago and—" She could not continue.

Nancy impulsively put an arm around Laura's shoulders. "I do understand," she said, and told of losing her own mother at the age of three.

Helen added, "Nancy lives with her father, a lawyer, and Hannah Gruen, their housekeeper."

"I'm an orphan," Laura stated simply. "My father was in a boat accident nearly six years ago." She explained that Mr. Pendleton's sailboat had capsized during a storm. He had been alone and no one had been near enough to save him.

"That's why," Laura added, "I knew I had to save whoever was crying for help on the lake today. I love to walk in a storm."

Nancy and Helen felt their hearts go out to the parentless girl. Not only was Laura brave, but also she showed great strength of character.

"With whom are you staying now?" Nancy asked Laura.

The girl looked troubled. "I'm alone at the moment. I checked in at the Montewago Hotel just this morning. But my guardian Jacob Aborn and his wife Marian are to arrive some time this evening. They're taking me to their summer home at Melrose Lake. I believe it's near here."

"Yes, it is," Nancy said.

"Do you know the Aborns?" Helen asked.

Laura said that she did not remember the couple. Her mother had frequently spoken of them, however.

"Mr. Aborn is distantly related to my mother, and it was her request that he become my legal guardian in case of her death."

Laura gave a slight sob, then went on, "But no answer came from our lawyer's letter to Mr. Aborn, who was traveling."

"How strange!" Nancy remarked.

"Finally I wrote to Mr. and Mrs. Aborn myself at the Melrose Lake address," Laura said. "The truth was I needed some money as a down payment on tuition at the boarding school I attend."

"And they replied?" Nancy asked.

"Yes. Mr. Aborn told me to come here and he and his wife would meet me."

Helen interrupted. "Then everything's settled, so you should be happy."

The girl shook her head. "I feel I'm not wanted. The letter wasn't cordial. Oh dear, what shall I do?"

Nancy gave Laura a hug. "You'll be at school and during vacations you can visit friends. And you have a new friend named Nancy Drew!"

"Oh, Nancy, you're sweet." Laura smiled for the first time, but in a moment her mood became sad again. "Living that way isn't like having your own home. Mother and I had such wonderful times together." She brushed away a few tears.

Nancy wanted to learn more but saw by her waterproof watch that it was six o'clock. Laura would have to hurry off to meet her guardian. The sky was getting lighter and the rain had almost stopped.

"We'd better leave," she suggested to Helen and Laura.

The girls washed the cups and saucepan, dressed, and put the blankets where they had found them. Before leaving the bungalow, Nancy wrote a note of thanks to the owner, signing it "Three grateful girls."

As they were parting, Laura said, "If my guardians don't arrive I'll call you and arrange a date for tomorrow."

"Please do!" Nancy and Helen urged, and waved good-by.

When they reached the Pinecrest Motel, the two girls went at once to talk to Mr. Franklin, the manager. They told him about the sunken motorboat, expressing extreme regret, and assured him that their parents would pay for the craft.

"Don't worry about that," the manager said. "We have insurance which takes care of such accidents. I'm just glad you girls are all right."

At that moment a short, thin woman swaggered into the office. Her print dress was mud-splattered and she had lost the heel to one shoe. Her wet, bleached hair clung to her head in an unbecoming fashion.

Ignoring Nancy and Helen, who were still conversing with Mr. Franklin, the woman said bluntly, "Is there anyone here who can change a tire for me? I just had a flat half a mile away."

"I'm afraid not," Mr. Franklin apologized. "I'm busy in the office and most of the help are off this evening."

"That's great!" the woman said angrily. "What am I supposed to do—walk to the Montewago Hotel? I'm late already!"

Although Nancy thought the stranded motorist was being extremely rude, she, nevertheless, suggested that the woman telephone a nearby service station. "I'm sure they'll send someone out to help you."

This idea was received with a snort as sparks of annoyance flashed in the woman's pale-blue eyes. "I'll think about that!" she said sarcastically, and, turning, limped toward the telephone booth. She banged the door shut behind her.

The three spectators looked after her with disgust and Helen said, "Some people don't deserve a helping hand."

The irate stranger was still in the booth when Nancy and Helen went off to their room on the ground floor. After a bath and change of clothes the girls felt better. A tasty dinner in the restaurant restored their energy and they played shuffleboard under the floodlights.

The next morning, as the two friends dressed, Helen asked, "Do you think Laura Pendleton will call us?" Helen was putting on Bermuda shorts and a candy-striped blouse.

"I imagine so," said Nancy, "unless her guardian and his wife took her to Melrose Lake last night."

"How far is that from here?" Helen inquired.

Nancy consulted a road map. "About twenty-five miles," she replied. Then, as she was putting on loafers, someone knocked on the door. Nancy went to see who it was.

Laura Pendleton stood in the doorway. She looked very pretty in a becoming pink cotton dress. But the girl's eyes were shadowed and she seemed highly distressed.

"Oh, Nancy—Helen!" Laura exclaimed. "I just had to come see you as soon as I could!"

"We're glad you did," Nancy said. "Come in." Before she could continue, Laura flung herself on Helen's bed and started to sob.

"What's wrong, Laura?" Nancy asked in concern, going over to her.

Slowly the girl sat up and wiped away her tears with a handkerchief. She apologized for her behavior, then said, "I don't think I'm going to be happy living with the Aborns—at least not with Mrs. Aborn!"

Troubled, Nancy asked Laura whether the guardian and his wife had arrived the evening before.

"Only Mrs. Aborn," Laura replied. "She came to my room about an hour after I left you girls.

She was wet and in a very nasty mood. Apparently she'd had a flat tire on the road and was delayed in getting help from some gasoline station."

Nancy and Helen exchanged significant glances. Mrs. Aborn sounded like the woman they had met in Mr. Franklin's office!

"What does your guardian's wife look like, Laura?" Helen asked with interest.

"She's blond, small, and thin. And I guess she was terribly upset about all the trouble she'd had. I understood this and tried to make her comfortable in the extra bedroom, but—"

Laura went on to say that Mrs. Aborn, instead of calming down, had become even more unpleasant, blaming the girl for making it necessary for her to drive to Twin Lakes in the bad storm.

"She said that Mary, my mother, had spoiled me and that I was going to have to toe the mark in her home— Oh, what will I do?" Laura asked.

Nancy did not know, but said Mrs. Aborn's behavior was inexcusable. Then she asked whether Laura's mother had known the guardian's wife well.

Instead of replying to the question, Laura said absently, "Mrs. Aborn called my mother 'Mary.' But, Nancy, Mother's name was Marie!"

CHAPTER III

Strange Guardians

NANCY was almost certain now that she and Helen had met the unpleasant Mrs. Aborn the night before. The woman's quarrelsome mood had extended to Laura.

Aloud Helen said, "But don't forget it's no fun to have car trouble on a bad night. That is apt to make anyone cross."

"I suppose so," Laura conceded.

"How was Mrs. Aborn this morning?" Nancy asked.

Laura's face brightened somewhat as she admitted that the woman had been pleasant and charming. "Mrs. Aborn apologized for her actions last night and said both she and her husband could hardly wait for me to come and live with them."

"I see," said Nancy, but with inward reservations.

"I guess I'm being foolish to worry." Laura smiled. "Mrs. Aborn did say she had met Mother only once, so that could explain the name mix-up."

"Where is Mr. Aborn?" Helen asked.

"He's arriving after lunch today. He was detained on business."

Nancy was puzzled. The Aborns' behavior was unusual and thoughtless, she felt.

"Mrs. Aborn is having her hair set at the beauty parlor in the hotel," Laura explained. "She suggested that I take a taxi here this morning if I felt I had to see you two—which I insisted I did," Laura said, grinning cheerfully.

Suddenly Nancy smiled. "I'm starved." She asked Laura to have a second breakfast with her and Helen in the motel restaurant.

"And afterward," Helen went on, "let's ask Marty Malone—the girl we met yesterday, Nancy —to make a foursome in tennis."

"Great!" said Laura to both suggestions.

When the three girls stepped outside, Nancy took a deep breath of air. She loved the earthy smell of the forests surrounding the lake resort, particularly the scent of the tall pines.

"What a day!" she exclaimed. Only a few fleecy white clouds broke the clear blue sky.

"The weatherman must be on our side." Helen chuckled.

A little later Nancy lent Laura tennis clothes, and the girls went to meet Marty Malone. Soon the four were playing a lively set on the courts located behind the motel. Laura and Nancy, who were partners, won. Helen and Marty took the second set.

"You're a terrific player, Nancy!" Laura exclaimed, as she scored a point during set three.

"Thanks," Nancy said, as they changed courts for service. "Where did you learn to play so well?"

"Private lessons." Laura grimaced. "At boarding school. Mother insisted. Before her illness she was a great sportswoman."

When Nancy and Laura had won the third set, Laura called for time out. "I must go back to the hotel now," she said. "It's almost noon."

After Laura had changed her clothes, Nancy offered to drive her to the hotel. The three girls piled into Nancy's blue convertible. Ten minutes later they drew up in front of the spacious Montewago Hotel. It was several stories high and stood a long distance back from the main road. In front stretched a green lawn bordered by beds of multi-colored gladioli, dahlias, and giant asters.

"It's beautiful!" Nancy commented, as Laura stepped from the car.

Helen pointed to an attractive outdoor swimming pool to the right of the hotel. It was filled with bathers. Laura said that there was also a riding stable behind the Montewago.

"There are a lot of families here," Laura said wistfully. "I wish I could stay." Then hastily she thanked Nancy for driving her over.

"I loved doing it," Nancy replied. "I hope we see each other again, Laura."

"So do I," Helen added.

Laura snapped her fingers. "I have a wonderful idea! Why don't you girls come back around three o'clock? You can meet my guardians. And if there's time, we can join the other young people at a tea dance scheduled for four."

"Fine!" Nancy said at once.

"Come directly to my room." Laura waved good-by.

Nancy detected a worried expression on Laura's face, and knew she hated the thought of meeting her strange new guardian.

The young sleuth was so quiet on the return trip that Helen said, "Penny for your thoughts, Nancy."

Her friend smiled. "I've concluded that the Pendletons must have been wealthy."

"What gives you that idea?"

"It's very expensive to live year round in New York hotels where Laura lived and she also mentioned boarding school. In addition," Nancy enumerated, "Laura's clothes have that simple but expensive look—you know what I mean."

"Yes," said Helen. "Well, if you're right, Mr. Aborn will control a great deal of money while he's managing Laura's affairs."

"In the case of a minor," said Nancy, "an inheritance is held in trust until she is twenty-one, Dad says. That's five years for Mr. Aborn. I hope he'll be a wise guardian."

She turned onto Lakeview Lane, a long, straight road bordered by woods. There were no homes along the way but a sign ahead advertised Sterling's real-estate office. Suddenly Nancy stopped.

"I think I'll run in here for a minute," she said, "and ask who owns that bungalow we helped ourselves to."

She walked into the office, introduced herself to Mr. Sterling, an elderly man, and told him the purpose of her call. The realtor grinned. "Any port in a storm is all right, I'm sure."

He said that the bungalow was owned by one of his clients. He had rented it a week before to a Mrs. Frank Marshall from Pittsburgh.

"I guess she fixed up the second floor," Mr. Sterling added. "She and her husband plan to use the place week ends. I'll pass the word along to Mrs. Marshall that you were there."

"I left a note but didn't sign it," Nancy said.

"Perhaps some time I'll stop in person and thank the Marshalls."

Returning to the car, she told Helen what she had learned. "Just for fun let's go out to the bungalow now."

A quarter of a mile farther on Nancy made a right-hand turn which brought them out on the lake drive. Below them, the girls could see the bungalow they had visited.

Suddenly a black foreign car pulled out of the lane that led down to the bungalow. Gaining speed, the automobile came toward Nancy's convertible.

"Watch out!" Helen yelled, jerking to attention as the vehicle passed and nearly sideswiped them.

Nancy slowed down and stopped. She looked back at the car which was almost out of sight. "Some drivers don't deserve a license," she said. "Do you suppose that was Mr. Marshall?"

Helen shrugged. "He wore a straw hat pulled low over his forehead. All I could see was the sleeve of his tan-and-white jacket."

"That's quite a bit," Nancy teased, "in so short a time."

Helen laughed. "Close association with you is making me more observant," she said.

When the girls reached the Pinecrest Motel, Helen exclaimed, "There's Aunt June!" While

Nancy parked, the dark-haired girl slipped from the convertible and hurried to the porch outside the room they occupied.

"Hello, Helen dear." The slim, stylishly dressed woman, with softly waved black hair, smiled at her niece.

Helen returned the greeting and gave her father's younger sister a kiss. "When did you arrive?" she asked. "Have you been waiting long?"

"No. I got here half an hour ago."

The attractive-looking woman was a buyer for a River Heights department store. She told Helen of a retailing problem which had prevented her departure with the girls, then turned to greet Nancy with enthusiasm.

"Isn't this a lovely spot?" Nancy remarked, and Aunt June Corning agreed that the view of the lake was superb.

After learning that Aunt June had not had lunch, the three went into the tearoom. When they had given their order, Miss Corning said, "I have some slightly bad news for you, Nancy."

"What's happened?"

"Well, just before I left River Heights, I phoned your housekeeper to see if she had any messages for you. To my surprise Dr. Darby answered. He said that Mrs. Gruen had sprained her ankle early this morning, and she must not walk for a couple of days."

"I'll call Dad right away and talk to him," said Nancy with concern.

"Wait!" Aunt June said. "Dr. Darby mentioned that your father left on a business trip today before the accident occurred."

"That means Hannah is all alone," Nancy said, rising. "I'll have to go home at once. Will you both excuse me for a minute, please?"

She went to a telephone booth and dialed the Drews' next-door neighbor, Mrs. Gleason. Nancy was relieved to hear that the woman's sister was taking care of Hannah for the afternoon. The housekeeper was in no pain and resting comfortably.

The young sleuth did some rapid thinking. If she left for River Heights late that afternoon she could still fulfill her promise to Laura to meet her guardian and arrive home in time to cook Hannah's supper.

"Will you please tell Mrs. Gruen I'll see her at six o'clock," Nancy requested, and Mrs. Gleason agreed to do this.

When Nancy returned to the others, Helen was telling her aunt of the adventure on the lake and Laura Pendleton's story.

"How dreadful for the girl!" exlaimed Miss Corning. "I feel very sorry for her."

Nancy now told of her plans to return home, and although Helen and her aunt were disappointed, they agreed that it was the right thing to do.

"But before I leave," said Nancy, "I want to meet Mr. and Mrs. Aborn."

After lunch Nancy packed her suitcase, put it in the car, and paid her motel bill. Soon it was time for her and Helen to leave for the Montewago Hotel.

"Are you sure you won't accompany us, Aunt June?" asked Helen.

Miss Corning shook her head. "I'm a little tired," she said, "and besides, I must unpack."

A short while later the two girls entered the Montewago lobby. Nancy made her way directly to the desk and after a brief wait was informed that Miss Pendleton would receive the girls in her suite. An elevator took them to the third floor.

Scarcely had they knocked on the door when Laura opened it. "Oh, I'm so glad you came," she cried out, smiling with relief.

Laura led the girls into a well-appointed living room with a bedroom on either side. As Nancy stepped inside, she saw a man and a woman seated in chairs near a picture window. In a glance Nancy realized that she and Helen had been right about Mrs. Aborn being the woman they had met the night before. Right now she looked more friendly.

Jacob Aborn arose and smiled graciously. He

was a well-built, somewhat stocky man in his early fifties. His face was square, and his small brown eyes were shifty.

When Laura introduced the girls, Mrs. Aborn rushed toward them. "Darlings!" she said, giving Helen and Nancy a butterfly peck on their cheeks. "You've been so good to poor Laura."

"Perfect bricks!" Mr. Aborn said gruffly. He extended a hand first to Nancy, then to Helen. "The reason I'm late in getting Laura is that I want everything to be perfect for her arrival at our Melrose Lake house."

Nancy was sure Mrs. Aborn recognized the callers and was embarrassed to admit it. They said nothing. There was an awkward silence until Laura said, "Well, let's all sit down."

For a few minutes everyone chatted generally, then Helen asked, "When are you leaving, Mr. Aborn?"

"In half an hour," was the reply. "Laura is tired and I want to get her settled before suppertime."

Mrs. Aborn broke in, "Yes, the poor child needs a lot of rest and good care."

Laura Pendleton seemed annoyed to be treated as a child and an invalid. "I'm fine," she stated defiantly. Turning to Nancy, she said quietly, "I'm afraid that we can't attend the hotel tea dance."

"That's all right," Nancy replied. She told of Hannah's accident and the fact that she must soon head for home.

"Are you all packed, Laura?" Mr. Aborn asked.

"Yes, except to get Mother's jewelry from the hotel safe."

"I'll do that for you, dear," Mrs. Aborn volunteered, rising. She smoothed her skirt restlessly.

Laura said, "Thank you, but I must present the receipt in person." She excused herself, saying she would be right back.

As Laura left the suite, Mr. Aborn turned to the two guests. "I wish Marie Pendleton had been a little more cautious with her inheritance from her husband," he confided.

"What do you mean?" Nancy asked.

"Laura is practically penniless," her guardian explained. "Mrs. Pendleton's illness and the way she lived took almost all her funds."

Nancy and Helen were surprised and dismayed to hear this.

"It doesn't matter, though," Mrs. Aborn said. "We have ample means to provide for Laura. She'll have everything she needs."

Nancy was confused by the woman's seemingly dual personality. She could be crude as on the evening before, or sweet as she appeared now. Perhaps, at heart, she meant well. Nancy hoped so for Laura's sake, but a strange feeling of distrust persisted.

When Laura returned, Helen and Nancy said they must be on their way. The friends shook hands.

"We never can thank you enough, Laura, for coming to our rescue yesterday," Helen said gratefully.

"That's right," Nancy agreed. "If you hadn't come along at that moment we'd probably be at the bottom of the lake!"

Laura shuddered. "Oh, I'm sure you would have reached shore some way! But I am glad I could help and it's been such fun knowing you. I hope you'll come to see me while I'm at Melrose Lake."

"We will," Nancy promised. "What is your address there?"

"Anyone can direct you to my house," Mr. Aborn said heartily. "It's well known in that section."

His wife tapped her foot on the floor. "Jacob, it's getting late," she hinted.

Nancy and Helen hastily bade the Aborns good-by and walked toward the door of the suite with Laura. Suddenly Helen turned around.

"It's lucky you brought two cars!" she called back. "Laura has a lot of luggage."

Without another word, Helen gave Laura a quick kiss and walked into the corridor. Nancy followed a moment later.

"Why did you say that?" Nancy questioned Helen as they rode down in the elevator.

The dark-haired girl signaled for silence. There were several other people in the car. When they stepped out into the lobby Nancy repeated her question.

Helen grabbed her chum's arm excitedly. "I couldn't resist it!" she exclaimed. "Jacob Aborn was the driver in the tan-and-white sports jacket I saw coming out of the road by the bungalow this morning! The driver of the black foreign car!"

CHAPTER IV

The Tree Crash

IF HELEN was right about Mr. Aborn's being the driver of the foreign car, then it should be in the hotel parking lot, Nancy thought.

"Let's take a look," she suggested.

The girls walked to the rear of the hotel where Nancy had left her own convertible. They scouted the lot. There was no sign of a black foreign car. Helen asked the attendant if one had been driven in that day. The man said no.

Helen was puzzled. "I was so sure I was right."

"You still could be," said Nancy. "The car may be parked somewhere else. Mrs. Aborn may have picked up her husband at some other point."

Puzzled, she and Helen climbed into the convertible and Nancy started the engine. As she drove back to the Pinecrest Motel, Helen remarked:

"I don't care for either Mr. or Mrs. Aborn. Their friendliness seems forced, and their promises don't ring true."

"I agree." Nancy nodded. "By the way, did you notice how Laura's guardian went out of his way to tell us she was penniless? And we were total strangers."

"I certainly did," Helen replied. "It was in very bad taste, I'd say."

"As soon as Hannah's ankle is better," Nancy declared, "I'm coming back here. Let's pay Laura a visit together at Melrose Lake. I feel very uneasy about her."

"A wonderful idea!" Helen exclaimed.

When they reached the motel, she got out. "I hope Hannah's foot improves quickly," she said, and waved Nancy out of sight.

A minute later Nancy was on the main highway which paralleled Twin Lakes for some distance. Presently, as she left the lake area, Nancy cast a speculative glance toward the sky. Did she imagine it or was it beginning to cloud over?

Nancy glanced at the speedometer. She was nearly halfway to River Heights. "Maybe I can get home before the storm breaks," she told herself.

A quarter of a mile farther on Nancy saw an obstruction in the road and brought the convertible to a halt. A huge sign read:

DETOUR. BRIDGE OUT. TAKE MELROSE LAKE ROAD. An arrow pointed to the left.

"Just when I'm in a hurry!" Nancy fumed, knowing she would have to go miles out of her way before reaching the River Heights road.

Another anxious glance at the sky told her there was no time to be lost. Already huge storm clouds were appearing.

"I'll be caught in another cloudburst like the one on the lake," she thought.

Hastily she headed the car down the Melrose Lake detour, a narrow, rutty road bordered with tall pines and thick shrubbery. Nancy was forced to reduce her speed to ten miles an hour, and even then it seemed as though the car would shake to pieces.

Within a few minutes it grew so dark that Nancy snapped on the headlights. Giant raindrops began to strike the windshield. In a short time they were followed by a blinding downpour, and the deep ruts in the road filled up like miniature streams.

"I'm in for it now," Nancy groaned, as the car crept up a hill.

Before she could reach a level stretch on the other side of the hill, the storm broke in all its fury. Trees along the roadside twisted and bent before the onslaughts of the rushing wind.

It was difficult for Nancy to see the road ahead.

She crawled along, endeavoring to keep the convertible's wheels out of deep ruts. As she swerved to avoid a particularly large puddle, a blinding tongue of lightning streaked directly in front of the car.

There was a flash of fire and simultaneously a deafening roar. For an instant, Nancy thought the car had been struck.

Almost blinded, the girl jammed on the brakes in time to hear a splintering, ripping noise. Before her horrified eyes a pine tree fell earthward. The convertible seemed to be directly in its line of fall!

"Oh!" Nancy gasped, as the tree missed her car by inches, landing directly in front of it.

Nancy felt as though she were frozen in her seat. How closely she had escaped possible death! When she was breathing normally again, Nancy ruefully surveyed the tree which blocked the road. What was she to do?

"I can't go back because the bridge is out," she told herself. "And there probably isn't anyone within miles of this place." She suddenly realized she had not seen another car going in either direction.

As Nancy continued to gaze at the fallen tree, she decided it could be moved by two people.

"Too bad I'm not twins," she thought. "I wonder how long it will be before someone comes past here."

Finally Nancy decided to try pulling the tree aside. She reached in the back seat for plastic boots and a raincoat with a hood. After putting these on, she stepped outside.

Gingerly picking her way through the mud and heavy rain, she walked to the fallen pine. She grasped the branches and tugged with all her might. The tree did not budge. Nancy next tried rolling it. This, too, she found was impossible.

"Oh, this is maddening," she thought, feeling completely frustrated.

As another low roll of thunder broke the quietness of the woods, Nancy was delighted to see headlights approaching. A moment later a small jeep pulled up behind her car.

The driver's door opened and a young man's voice said, "Hello there! Having trouble?"

"I sure am," said Nancy, as he walked toward her and stood outlined in the convertible's headlights. He appeared to be about seventeen, had dark hair, and twinkling eyes. Quickly Nancy explained about the fallen tree.

"Wow! You were lucky that it missed you!" the boy cried, then added, "It will be easy for the three of us to move the tree."

"Three?" Nancy questioned.

He laughed. "My sister's in the jeep," he explained, then called out, "Come on out, Cath!"

They were joined by a pretty girl, whom Nancy guessed to be fourteen years old. Introductions were exchanged. The brother and sister were Jim and Cathy Donnell. They lived off the next main highway and were returning home from visiting friends.

"I'm glad we came by," Cathy said. "There's only one house on this road and the people haven't moved in yet for the summer."

After Jim had pulled some tangled pine branches away from the convertible, he and the two girls were able to lift the trunk. Little by little they moved the tree far enough aside so that the cars could drive ahead.

"I'll report this to the highway patrol when we get home," said Jim.

"Thanks so much for your help," Nancy told the brother and sister. "By the way, do you know a Mr. and Mrs. Aborn who live at Melrose Lake?"

"We certainly do," said Cathy. "They're the ones whose house is on this route. It's a lovely place, with a lane leading to the house. You passed it about a mile back. The Aborns just bought the place."

"It's a small world," Nancy observed. She told the Donnells, however, that they were wrong

Nancy tried to pull the fallen tree aside

about the Aborns not being at their home, and explained about meeting the couple and Laura Pendleton at Twin Lakes.

"That's funny," said Jim. He explained that his parents had known the Aborns for years. "They used to have a place on the other side of the larger lake, and bought this new house only a month ago. They mentioned that Laura Pendleton was coming to visit them, but said they were taking an extensive trip first."

"I see," said Nancy, thinking, "Another strange angle to this thing!" Aloud she asked, "Is Mrs. Aborn a blond-haired woman, rather small and slight, Cathy?"

"Yes."

Jim said that he and Cathy must say good-by. Their parents would be worried if they did not arrive home soon.

"We'll tell Mother and Dad about the Aborns and Laura," said Jim. "We're all keen to meet Laura. The Aborns think she must be tops!"

"And we want to introduce Laura to our friends here at the lake," Cathy added.

"Grand!" Nancy said enthusiastically. "Laura has had a pretty sad time recently. She needs friends."

The three said good-by and got into their own cars. As Nancy drove on, she kept mulling over the Aborn-Pendleton enigma. She inferred from the Donnells' remarks that the man and his wife were very acceptable people. But Nancy certainly had not received this impression of them.

"I can't wait to meet them again," she thought, "and see how they're treating Laura."

By the time Nancy reached the end of the detour, the storm was over. A little later she turned into the Drews' driveway and parked near the front porch of the large red-brick house. She climbed from the car and made a dash for the porch with her suitcase.

As she inserted her key in the lock and pushed the front door open, a voice called out from the living room, "Nancy? Is that you?"

"Yes, Hannah. Be right in."

Nancy took off her raincoat and boots and put them in the vestibule closet. Then she hurried into the living room and hugged the motherly-looking woman, who was reclining on the sofa.

"Hannah! I'm so sorry about your ankle. How are you feeling?"

A worried expression faded from the housekeeper's face as she said, "I'm fine, now that you're home. This storm has been dreadful and I was concerned about you being on the road. Helen phoned that you were on your way."

Nancy told of the fallen tree at Melrose Lake, and how it had taken her longer than she had planned to make the trip.

"Goodness!" the housekeeper exclaimed. Then she smiled. "Nancy, you're like a cat with nine lives, the way you so often just miss being injured."

Nancy laughed. Then, becoming serious, she asked, "Where did Dad go?"

"To the state capital," Hannah replied, "and that reminds me, dear—you're to call Mr. Drew at eight tonight—" She gave Nancy a slip of paper with a telephone number on it.

"Did he say what he wanted?" Nancy inquired.

A look of concern appeared on Hannah's face as she said, "Mr. Drew wishes you to help him with an embezzlement case he's investigating!"

CHAPTER V

The Unexpected Prowler

AN EMBEZZLEMENT case! Nancy was excited. What, she wondered, did her father want her to do? The young detective longed to place a call to him immediately, but knew she must wait until eight o'clock.

"Where is Mrs. Gleason's sister?" she asked.

Hannah said that the woman had left a short while before, after hearing that Nancy would be home by suppertime.

"But first she fixed a chicken casserole dish for us," Hannah added. "It's all ready to pop in the oven. My dear, I hate to bother you—"

Nancy grinned mischievously and teased, "You mean you hate to have anyone else but you reign in your kitchen. Don't worry, Hannah, I'll be neat."

"Oh posh!" said Hannah. She blushed and gave Nancy a loving glance.

Humming softly, Nancy went to the modern pink-and-white kitchen. The casserole, which looked tempting, stood on one of the gleaming counter tops. After lighting the oven, Nancy placed the dish inside to heat.

She set two wooden trays with doilies, napkins, and silver. Then, after placing bread and butter on each, Nancy poured two glasses of milk. Lastly, she made a crisp salad of lettuce and tomatoes and marinated it with a tangy French dressing.

While waiting for the casserole, Nancy went back to the living room. Hannah was reading the evening paper.

"You're a wonderful help, dear," the house-keeper said gratefully, looking up. "Tell me, did you enjoy your vacation?"

"It was lovely," said Nancy, and described the resort. She then told Hannah of the adventure on Twin Lakes and of Laura Pendleton and the Aborns.

"Hannah, wouldn't it be nice if Laura could visit us sometime soon?"

"It certainly would."

By now their supper was ready and Nancy brought it in on the trays. After they had eaten, she put the dishes in the washer, then helped Hannah, who was using crutches, upstairs to bed.

Nancy then went out to put her car in the garage, and returned to the house just as the clock was striking eight. She went to place the call to Carson Drew.

Nancy looked at the series of numbers on the slip of paper Hannah had given her:

942 HA 5–4727

She dialed the long-distance number, and after one brief ring the phone on the other end was picked up.

"Hotel Williamston," the switchboard operator answered.

"May I speak with Mr. Carson Drew?" his daughter requested.

"One moment, please."

There was a pause, then the operator's voice said, "I'm sorry but Mr. Drew checked out this evening."

"Did he say where he was going?" Nancy inquired in amazement.

The desk clerk said no. Nancy thanked him and hung up, feeling oddly upset. It was unlike her father to change his plans without calling home to tell where he would be. Could anything have happened to him? she wondered.

Since Hannah was asleep, Nancy did not awaken her to discuss the matter. Leaving on a light in the lower hall, she went to her own room and unpacked, deep in thought. As she hung up her dresses in the closet the young sleuth wondered if her father might be following a new clue in another city.

Deciding that this probably was what had happened and that she would hear from her father the next morning, Nancy felt reassured, took a bath, and went to bed. She fell asleep almost immediately.

Several hours later Nancy was awakened by the sound of a dull thud. She sat up and groped for the bedside light. Turning it on, she got out of bed and slipped into her robe and slippers.

"I hope Hannah hasn't fallen out of bed," Nancy thought worriedly, and hurried down the carpeted hall to the housekeeper's room.

Peering in the bedroom door, Nancy saw that Hannah was sound asleep. Puzzled, Nancy went back to her own room. The girl detective had almost decided she had been dreaming, then she heard an even louder noise.

The creaky window in the ground-floor library was being opened! Someone was entering the house!

Alarmed, Nancy decided to call the police and tiptoed to the bedside telephone in Mr. Drew's room. When the sergeant answered, she told him she would unlock the front door.

Nancy tiptoed quietly down the stairs. Upon reaching the ground floor, she eyed the closed door of the library, located at the far end of the living room. Not a sound came from the library which Mr. Drew used as a study.

With bated breath Nancy moved toward the front door and opened it. At that instant the library door was flung open. A man's dark figure was outlined in the doorway. Nancy's heart skipped three beats.

As Nancy debated whether to run outdoors or upstairs, she heard a loud chuckle. At the same time, a table lamp was turned on.

"Dad!" cried Nancy in disbelief, as color flooded back into her face. "Is it really you?"

"Of course!" said Carson Drew, a tall, distinguished-looking man who right now seemed a little sheepish.

He placed the brief case he was carrying on a table, then walked toward Nancy with outstretched arms. His daughter rushed into them and gave Mr. Drew a loving kiss.

"You're the best-looking burglar I've ever seen!" Nancy declared, and told her father of fearing the house was being entered. Then she clapped a hand to her face. "The police! I notified the police when I heard the window creaking open."

At that very moment father and daughter heard a car stop outside. Two policemen rushed in.

"Where's the burglar?"

"Right here," Mr. Drew confessed. "I forgot my house key. Sorry to put you to this trouble."

The policemen grinned and one said, "I wish all our burglary cases were solved this easy!" A few minutes later the officers left.

Mr. Drew explained to Nancy that he had hesitated about ringing the doorbell and disturbing Mrs. Gruen and Nancy. Recalling that one of the windows in the library did not close completely and needed repair, he removed the screen and opened the window.

"I'm sorry I scared you. I flew home tonight rather unexpectedly and didn't have a chance to let you know, Nancy."

"Has there been a new development in your embezzlement case, Dad?" she inquired.

Mr. Drew nodded. "Yes, but since it's late I suggest we both go to bed. We can talk about it in the morning."

Nancy stifled a yawn. "Good idea," she agreed.

Father and daughter turned off the lights and went upstairs. Both slept soundly until eight o'clock the following morning when Nancy was awakened by Hannah.

"Get up, sleepyhead!" said the housekeeper. Teasingly she prodded Nancy's foot with the tip of a wooden crutch while leaning on another one. "It's a beautiful day!"

Nancy jerked awake, rubbing her eyes. "Hannah!" she gasped. "What are you doing up?"

The housekeeper smiled. "One day of staying off my feet will keep me well for a year," she declared. "Besides, I feel fine this morning."

"But Dr. Darby said—" Nancy began.

"Stuff and nonsense!" Hannah replied tartly. "He left me these crutches to use and that's what I intend to do with them. Nancy, is your father home? I noticed his door is closed."

"Yes, Hannah." Nancy related the burglar scare.

The housekeeper smiled in amusement. Then, with a swish of her skirt, she turned and clumped out of the room. She paused at the door, winked at Nancy, and said:

"Pancakes and sausage at eight-thirty—and you tell your dad that I'm going to squeeze some extra-juicy oranges."

Mr. Drew was awake also. Nancy could hear the buzz of his electric razor! It was good, she thought, for the little family to be home again.

In half an hour they were seated in the cheerful breakfast room. As they began to eat, Mr. Drew caught up on the latest news and listened with concern to the story of Nancy's two storm adventures.

"I'm grateful that you're here safely beside me," he said gravely.

When the lawyer heard about Laura Pendleton and the Aborns, he frowned. "I agree with you, Nancy, it does sound strange," he said. "But you should not interfere with Laura and her guardians unless she asks you to. They may turn out to be very nice people."

"I agree," said Hannah, then added pointedly, "But if things should prove otherwise, Mr. Drew?"

"Then I'd be happy to help Laura have another guardian appointed by the court," the lawyer replied. "In the meantime, Nancy, let's invite Laura to spend a few days with us very soon."

Nancy beamed. "Thanks, Dad. That's just what I wanted to do."

When the meal was finished and the dishes had been put in the washer, Mr. Drew and Nancy went to his study, a comfortable room with book-lined shelves, deep-seated leather chairs, and a wide, highly polished mahogany desk.

Nancy sat down in a yellow club chair, then said eagerly, "Come on, Dad, don't hold out on me any longer about this case of yours."

Mr. Drew smiled, and absently fingered a glass paperweight. Sitting down, he began to talk.

Mr. Drew's client, a Mr. Seward, was the president of the Monroe National Bank in Monroe. It had branches throughout the country, including one in River Heights. During a recent audit, many valuable securities had been discovered missing from the main bank's vault. Most of the securities were bonds which read "Payable to Bearer."

"How dreadful!" said Nancy. "It means that whoever has the bonds can cash them."

"That's right." Mr. Drew said that the bonds belonged to various bank clients throughout the country. In all cases the clients had inherited money and had asked the bank as custodian to invest it for them. A Mr. Hamilton was put in charge. This was a very common bank procedure: the bank made the investments and paid the dividends to the individual, thus relieving the person of handling his own transactions.

"I was called in on the case," Carson Drew said, "by Mr. Sill, manager of our River Heights branch, when Mr. Seward advised him that a number of the missing securities belong to residents in our community. Mr. Seward felt this was an odd coincidence."

"It is," Nancy agreed. "Have you any idea who might have taken the property?"

Mr. Drew said no. So far the evidence pointed to Mr. Hamilton, although the man was a highly trusted officer.

"What about the people who work in the vault?" Nancy asked, wrinkling her forehead.

"They're being checked on now. Most of these

employees have worked for the bank a long time, however. At present two of them are on vacation, so the investigation may take some time."

"Couldn't you find out where they went?" Nancy asked.

"We've tried that," her father replied, "but they're not at their homes and the neighbors don't know where they're vacationing. We'll just have to wait until the men get home."

"I see," Nancy agreed.

"The main thing is," said Mr. Drew, "that Mr. Seward doesn't want any publicity about the theft. The bank will continue to pay dividends to the security holders, of course. My assignment is to find the missing property and the guilty person."

"A big order," said Nancy. "How are you going to do this?"

Carson Drew said he was presently checking on employees other than Hamilton who worked in the custodian department. Also, he was trying to find out if there might be a tie-in between the thief and one or more of the persons whose property was missing.

"There must be several people behind this theft," the lawyer explained. "It's pretty difficult in these times to rob a bank, with all the security measures they employ. Nothing is impossible, however, if a plan is well worked out."

"Sounds like an exciting case, Dad," said Nancy. "What can I do to help?"

In reply Mr. Drew gave Nancy a slip of paper with four names on it and their corresponding River Heights addresses. They were: Mrs. William Farley, Mr. Herbert Brown, Mrs. John Stewart, Mr. Stephen Dowd. None of the names was familiar to the young detective.

"These are the local people whose securities are missing," Mr. Drew said. "Think of some reason to meet these people," he directed. "See what kind of homes they have, and try to get an insight into their characters. This is a very vague assignment, but I feel you may find out something incriminating about one of them—you see, we have to be very careful not to arouse suspicion in a case of this type."

"I'll do my best," Nancy assured him.

"The out-of-town names I'll check myself," her father explained. "They live in various large cities around the country, so I'll have to be away a good bit during the next few weeks."

"I'll get busy on these names right away," Nancy said. She gave her father a quick hug. "You're an old dear to let me help you!"

"Promise me you'll be careful," the lawyer warned. "An embezzler can be a dangerous person. And in this case whoever is behind the thefts is playing for big stakes."

The young sleuth said she would take every precaution. As Nancy stood up, the telephone rang.

"I'll get it, Dad," she offered, and hurried to pick up the receiver of the hall phone.

A low-pitched feminine voice said tersely, "Nancy? Nancy Drew?"

"Yes. This is Nancy speaking."

As she held on, waiting for the caller's identification, she heard sounds of a scuffle on the other end of the receiver. This was followed by a cry of pain and a loud *crash!*

CHAPTER VI

An Invitation to Sleuth

"Who is this?" Nancy asked.

But the caller had cut off the connection. What had happened to her? Nancy wondered. Certainly she had sounded very distressed. Nancy hung up and waited for a second call, but the phone did not ring.

"Who was it?" Mr. Drew asked, coming into the hall.

Nancy told what had occurred.

"You didn't recognize the voice?" he remarked.

"No, so I can't call back. Oh dear, someone is in trouble, I just know it. And here I stand helpless to do a thing! It's maddening!"

"It certainly is," her father said. "Well, dear, I must run down to the office." Presently he left the house.

After seeing that Hannah was comfortable, Nancy went to her bedroom and thoughtfully opened the closet door.

"This is as good a day as any to start Dad's investigation," she thought.

Nancy took out a two-piece navy-blue dress which made her look older than her eighteen years. Next, she found a pair of comfortable low-heeled pumps.

For several minutes Nancy experimented with various hair styles. She finally chose a simple off-the-face arrangement. Nancy put on tiny pearl earrings, dusted her nose lightly with powder, and finally added a dash of lipstick.

After she had changed her clothes and given herself a final appraisal, Nancy went to Hannah's room to tell her she was going out for a while.

"Gracious, Nancy," said the housekeeper, giving the girl a sharp glance, "you look awfully businesslike today. Where are you going?"

"Dad asked me to look up something for him," she said. "I'll be back in time for lunch."

"Don't worry about that," said Hannah. "I can get around. Have a good time, dear."

When Nancy left the house she consulted the list Mr. Drew had given her. Mrs. William Farley, the first name on the paper, lived on Acorn Street, seven blocks from the Drew residence.

Nancy set out at a brisk pace, rehearsing in her

mind the approach on which she had decided. One of the girl's favorite community projects was a recreational youth center located in downtown River Heights. The center always needed volunteer helpers as well as entertainers for the children.

"A good way to find out something about Dad's suspects," Nancy decided, "is to see how they will respond to a needy cause. And I'll be telling the truth when I say that I'm working for the organization."

This resolved, Nancy soon reached a modest white house which was set back from the street a short distance. The front walk was outlined with pink and white petunias and the grass was well tended.

Nancy rang the bell. The door was opened almost immediately by an elderly woman with wavy white hair and the greenest, most alert, eyes Nancy had ever seen.

"Yes?" she inquired pleasantly.

Nancy introduced herself, then explained the purpose of her call. She was invited inside.

"Please be seated," said the woman, sitting down herself. Nancy chose a Duncan Phyfe rocking chair covered with a black floral print.

The hostess smiled. "I'd be glad to help you with your project, my dear," she said, "although I have no talent. Also, I don't leave this house very much. I'm a recent widow, you see, and I haven't been too well lately."

Nancy expressed sympathy and said she understood completely. She liked this friendly little woman on first sight.

"Would a small check help your cause?" the widow asked. "Perhaps you could buy some equipment for the children."

"That would be wonderful," Nancy said. "But I'm not soliciting funds."

Mrs. Farley smiled shyly. "I realize this," she said. "But there's so little I can do to help others. Mr. Farley left most of his estate, which was modest, in trust. And I have only a tiny income to live on."

The woman arose, and despite Nancy's protests, went to the desk where she wrote out a check.

Nancy thanked her profusely, for she realized that this was a sacrifice on the widow's part.

"I'm glad I can help," said Mrs. Farley. "Please come see me again and tell me how the youth center is coming along."

Nancy promised to do this. After a few more minutes of conversation, she bade Mrs. Farley good-by and left the house.

"If I'm a judge of human nature," thought Nancy, "that woman never did a mean thing in her life!"

When she reached the sidewalk, Nancy took out Mr. Drew's list from her handbag. Thoughtfully she crossed out Mrs. Farley's name.

Herbert Brown, the next suspect, lived in River Heights Estates, a rather exclusive housing area located on the outskirts of the city.

"It's kind of a long walk," Nancy told herself. "But it will do me good."

As Nancy strolled along, she was so engrossed with her thoughts that she failed to notice a tan sedan whose driver cruised by, honked the horn, then pulled over to the curb.

As the door opened, a good-looking young man about eighteen called, "Hi, Nancy!"

To her surprise, she saw Don Cameron, who had been a fellow student in River Heights High School. Nancy had, in fact, gone to the Spring Prom with the tall, black-haired boy.

"Hello, Don," she said. "What are you doing home? I thought you were working on your uncle's farm this summer before going to college."

Don grinned engagingly. "I've been picking string beans and berries and hoeing potatoes for nearly a month," he replied. "But I have a leave of absence to attend my sister's wedding this Friday."

Nancy had read of Janet Cameron's wedding plans in the *River Heights Gazette* two weeks before. "Jan must be excited!" she exclaimed.

"Everyone at home is going 'round in circles," Don stated, laughing. "Bill Bent, my brother-in-law-to-be, is no better.

"By the way, Nancy," Don continued, "I intended calling you later today. If you're free Thursday afternoon and evening I'd like to have you go to a barbecue party with me. It's being given in honor of Jan and Bill."

"I'd love to," said Nancy. "Where will it be?"

"At the Herbert Browns' home in River Heights Estates," Don said. "Their daughter, Lynn, is Jan's maid of honor."

Herbert Brown! One of the possible suspects in the bank security theft! Nancy could scarcely conceal her excitement. Although she did not like the idea of spying on a host, here was an excellent chance for her to find out what Mr. Brown was like.

"What time does the barbecue begin?" Nancy asked.

"I'll call for you at four," said Don.

He offered to drive Nancy home, and she hopped in beside him. When the young sleuth entered the house, she found Hannah in the living room.

"My goodness," the housekeeper exclaimed, "you haven't solved the mystery already!"

"I gave up," Nancy teased.

"What!"

With a grin Nancy told why she had postponed her trip. "I'll get some lunch for us," Nancy offered, "and then drive to the other two places on the list."

Hannah chuckled. "Since you said you'd be home," she said, "I prepared a fresh fruit salad— it's in the refrigerator. And rolls ready to pop into the oven."

"You're a fine patient!" Nancy scolded.

"I feel better keeping busy," Hannah countered.

Nancy asked whether there had been any telephone calls in her absence.

"No. But you did get a post card in the mail."

Nancy went to the mail tray in the hall and recognized Helen Corning's writing. The message read:

Dear Nancy:

Aunt June and I have decided to take a week's automobile trip up North. Will return directly to River Heights. Plan to stop and see Laura Pendleton on our way. Hope Hannah is better.

Love,
Helen

Nancy read the card aloud and commented, "I hope Helen lets me know how everything is at the Aborns' home. Anyway, I'm going to call

Laura myself in a few days to find out how she is and make a date with her to come here."

"Do you think her guardian will let her leave his care so soon?" the housekeeper asked, as she reached for her crutches.

When there was no reply, Hannah looked out toward the hall. Nancy's normally rosy complexion was deadly white. She looked as if she were about to faint!

CHAPTER VII

A Startling Assignment

"Nancy! Nancy! What's wrong with you?" Hannah cried out, as she tried to hurry to the girl's side.

As the housekeeper limped toward her, Nancy snapped to attention. "I'm all right, Hannah," she said. "But Helen's post card—it brought back the phone call I had this morning—"

Nancy told Mrs. Gruen about the call which had ended so abruptly with a cry of pain. "The caller's voice sounded vaguely familiar, but I couldn't place it," she explained. "Now I think I know who it was."

"Who?" said Hannah.

"Laura Pendleton! I believe someone was trying to stop her from talking to me!"

"Mercy!" Hannah exclaimed, sinking weakly into a soft chair. "Do you think it was one of the

Aborns, Nancy? And why would they do such a thing?"

Nancy shrugged. "I'm going to call the Aborn home right now."

While Hannah listened nervously, Nancy picked up the phone and dialed Information. When the operator replied, Nancy asked for Jacob Aborn's number.

The operator cut off for a minute, then reported, "I'm sorry, miss, but that number has been temporarily disconnected!"

"Can you tell me when this was done?" Nancy requested tersely.

"I'm sorry. I have no further information."

Nancy thanked the operator and hung up.

"It sounds suspicious," Hannah remarked, "but, Nancy, the Aborns may have changed their plans and gone away with Laura for a vacation somewhere else."

"I know one way to find out," said Nancy with determination. She reminded Hannah of the young couple, Cathy and Jim Donnell, who had helped move the fallen tree at Melrose Lake.

"I'll ask them if they've seen Laura or the Aborns," Nancy explained.

Hannah sighed. "You're just like your father," she said, "and he certainly is astute. But I'm worried that you're becoming involved in another complicated mystery."

Nancy tweaked Hannah's cheek. "The more there are, the better I like them!"

The housekeeper smiled. She said that while Nancy was calling Cathy and Jim she would put lunch on the table.

"Fine. I'll help you in a moment."

As Hannah hobbled to the kitchen, Nancy got the Donnells' number and dialed it. After two rings a girl's voice said, "Hello!"

"Cathy?" Nancy inquired.

"Yes."

Nancy gave her name. "Do you remember me?" she asked.

"Of course," said Cathy. "My family and I were talking about you just a short while ago. Jim and I told them about the Aborns' being home and we all went over this morning to say hello and meet Laura. But the house was closed. Nobody's staying there."

"Oh!" said Nancy, disappointed. She explained that this was her reason for calling, and told of the Aborns' telephone having been disconnected.

Cathy already knew this, and added, "Dad found a note on the back porch telling the milk-man to discontinue deliveries until further notice."

"Cathy, does Mr. Aborn own a foreign make of car?" Nancy queried.

"Why, no," Cathy replied. She added that her

parents thought the Aborns might have planned suddenly to take a short trip somewhere. "I'm sure that we'll hear from them in a few days. If we do, I'll call you, Nancy."

"Fine," said the young detective. "Remember me to Jim. Good-by."

Deeply troubled, Nancy went to the kitchen and told Hannah what Cathy had said.

"Chances are," said the housekeeper, "the call you received this morning was not from Laura at all. You know a lot of people, dear."

Nancy replied that usually when someone had to break a telephone conversation in an abrupt manner the person called back as soon as possible to explain what had happened.

"That's true," Hannah admitted. "It's very strange."

After lunch Hannah said she was going next door to visit with Mrs. Gleason. Nancy helped her to the neighbor's front porch. Then Nancy backed her convertible from the garage and headed for Mr. Drew's downtown office.

"I'll report my progress so far regarding his suspects."

Nancy parked the car in a lot adjoining a large building where lawyers, doctors, and other professional people had offices. Mr. Drew's suite was on the fifth floor. A few minutes later Nancy greeted her father's secretary, Miss Hanson.

"My, how pretty you look, Nancy!" said the efficient young woman, who had been with Carson Drew for the past five years.

"Thank you." Nancy blushed a trifle. "You look lovely yourself."

When the lawyer learned that his daughter had arrived, Carson Drew at once asked Nancy to come into his office.

"I can see by the gleam in your eyes, Nancy, that you have some information for me."

Nancy told him of her interview with Mrs. Farley. "In my opinion, she's a woman of very fine character." Then Nancy mentioned the invitation to the barbecue party at Mr. Herbert Brown's home.

Mr. Drew raised his eyes and chuckled. "Better than I expected."

"My main reason for coming was to tell you something else," Nancy said.

She quickly reviewed the latest developments in the Laura Pendleton case. Mr. Drew listened quietly. Finally he said:

"There's something odd about all this. Nancy, I must leave River Heights on the three-o'clock plane this afternoon for Cincinnati, but I'll be home by Sunday. Why don't we plan to drive to the Aborns' home later that afternoon and see for ourselves what the story is? They may have returned by then."

"That's a grand idea!" Nancy exclaimed. Then, knowing that he was busy, she kissed her father good-by and wished him a successful trip.

"I'll call you every night at eight!" Mr. Drew promised, and Nancy left the office.

On the way down in the elevator, Nancy asked Hank, the operator, if he knew where Hilo Street was located. Mrs. John Stewart, the third suspect, lived in an apartment at this address.

"I know the general area," Nancy added. "It's about three miles from here on the eastern side of the city."

"That's right," Hank said. "It's a classy neighborhood! All high-priced apartment buildings. I believe Hilo Street runs off East Main."

Nancy thanked him, then went to her convertible. She drove carefully through the city traffic and finally reached Hilo Street. Mrs. Stewart's apartment house was Number 76.

Nancy scanned the buildings and found that this one was the largest on the street. It was ultramodern in design and about twenty stories high. After parking her car, she smoothed her hair and got out.

A red-coated doorman nodded pleasantly to the young detective as she entered the building a minute later. Nancy checked the directory and saw that Mrs. Stewart was in Apartment Three on the fourth floor. She rang the elevator button.

Almost instantly, aluminum doors slid open noiselessly, and Nancy stepped inside the carpeted elevator. It was self-operated, and Nancy pushed the fourth-floor control.

Her heart was pounding with excitement. Would Mrs. Stewart prove to be a link in the embezzlement case? Nancy hoped to find a clue this time!

When the elevator stopped at the fourth floor, Nancy got out and easily located Apartment Three. She pressed the doorbell.

A trim-looking maid, a rather harassed expression on her pretty face, opened the door immediately. "Oh, hello!" she said. "You must be the walker."

"Why, no—" Nancy began, but before she could explain, the maid went into the living room, leaving the door ajar.

As Nancy, speechless, glanced hastily into the apartment beyond, the maid reappeared. She was leading a pair of frisky black-and-white French poodles by a gold-linked leash.

"Here!" she said abruptly, thrusting the leash into Nancy's hand. "Their names are Irene and Frederika. Mrs. Stewart says to take them for a nice, long walk!"

Before Nancy could utter a word, the door was closed with an emphatic bang!

CHAPTER VIII

The Frightened Runaway

NANCY DREW, dog tender! This was a new title, the young detective thought. As she burst into laughter, the two poodles began to yap excitedly and dance around in little circles.

"Hello, girls," Nancy said to them, and bent down to pat the friendly animals. She then rang the doorbell with determination.

This time the door was opened by a tremendously stout woman whose chubby face was framed by a mass of fuzzy brown curls.

"Yes?" she inquired coyly. "Have you had some trouble with the babies? I told Collette to give you explicit instructions."

Nancy smothered a giggle. "Are you Mrs. Stewart?" she asked briskly.

"Of course," the woman said impatiently.

Nancy introduced herself and said that a mistake had been made. She was not the dog walker, but had come to solicit Mrs. Stewart's aid for the River Heights Youth Center.

"Oh dear!" Mrs. Stewart blushed, obviously flustered. "Collette's made a mistake. I'm sorry." She jerked the leash from Nancy and gave the poodles a loving glance. "Mama will give you both cookies while we wait for your real walker."

Nancy cleared her throat and Mrs. Stewart's glance returned to the caller. "Oh, yes—your project. I'm afraid that we'll have to discuss it another time. I'm having an afternoon musicale featuring the most divine violinist—Professor Le Bojo. He is expected any moment—"

"I understand," Nancy nodded. "Perhaps I can return later when Mr. Stewart is home?"

"He left today for a fishing trip in Maine," Mrs. Stewart replied. She added somewhat angrily, "I simply don't understand Gerald—he doesn't appreciate our home life here with the children!" Her glance swept toward the poodles.

Nancy managed to keep a straight face, said good-by to Mrs. Stewart, and left. When she returned to her car Nancy reached the conclusion that Mrs. Stewart was hardly the type to plan a bank swindle!

"Her poor husband," Nancy thought with a laugh.

There was only one more name for Nancy to check today—Mr. Stephen Dowd. She drove out Hilo Street and headed across the city. The man's address was in a business zone which was partly residential, although most of the homes were two-family dwellings.

After a little difficulty, Nancy found the house she sought—a brown duplex situated between a gasoline station and a tailor shop. She parked and went up the walk. Mr. Dowd's half of the house was on the right-hand side.

The young sleuth rang the bell and waited. No answer. She pushed the button again. Still no one came to the door.

"Maybe I can find out something from his next-door neighbor," Nancy thought hopefully.

As she was about to ring the bell on the left, the door was opened by a young woman, a shopping bag in her hand. She appeared startled to see Nancy.

The young sleuth smiled pleasantly. "I came to call on Mr. Dowd," she explained. "He's probably at work?"

"No. Mr. and Mrs. Dowd are both away now—on tour with a show, they said. They board here. I'm Mrs. Wyman."

"Are they entertainers?" Nancy inquired with interest, and explained about the youth center.

Mrs. Wyman said the couple were actors, but

she did not know what parts they played. "Since moving here two months ago, they've been away a great deal of the time."

Nancy thanked Mrs. Wyman and said she would call again. "They sound like the type of people I'm looking for to help amuse the children," she explained.

Nancy drove away, but told herself they would bear further investigation. It seemed unnatural that they would not have told what parts they were playing.

Nancy felt a little discouraged about her findings so far. She realized that she could do nothing else until she met Herbert Brown the next afternoon.

"I think I'll go home, get my bathing suit, and head for the club," she decided. The day was becoming very warm.

Fifteen minutes later Nancy parked in her driveway. As she was about to insert her key in the front lock, the door was opened from inside.

Laura Pendleton, wan and disheveled, stared at the young detective!

"Laura!" Nancy gasped. She could hardly believe her eyes.

"Hello, Nancy," her friend said, as Hannah Gruen came into view, walking slowly on her crutches.

"Come in, Nancy," the housekeeper invited

urgently. "Laura's been waiting for you over an hour. She's terribly upset—"

The three went into the living room and Nancy sat down on the couch beside the visitor. Before Nancy could ask why she was in River Heights, Laura burst into tears.

"Oh, I'm so unhappy!" she sobbed. "That's why I ran away!"

Nancy gently stroked Laura's hair and waited for the hysterical girl to calm down. Then she said quietly, "Tell me everything that has happened since I saw you last."

Slowly Laura started to speak. After Nancy and Helen had left the hotel suite, Mr. Aborn said he had to attend to some business for a short while. He had left the hotel. Meanwhile, Laura and Mrs. Aborn had checked out and waited for the guardian in his blue sedan, which was parked in the hotel lot.

"Where did Mr. Aborn go?" asked Nancy.

"I don't know, but when he met us a short while later he was carrying a brief case. As we started toward Melrose Lake, Mrs. Aborn asked what I had done with Mother's jewelry. When I said it was in my handbag she asked me to give it to her for safekeeping. I said I would when we got home."

"Then you *did* go directly to Melrose Lake?" Nancy questioned.

"Yes," Laura replied. She hesitated, then went on with her story. "The Aborns showed me to my room and I started to unpack.

"I found I needed more hangers," the girl went on, "but when I went to the door to ask Mrs. Aborn for them, I discovered it was locked on the outside."

"Locked!" Hannah gasped and Nancy was shocked.

Laura nodded. "I was so frightened," she said, "that at first I didn't know what to do. Then I heard voices coming from the Aborns' room. I lay down on the floor so I could hear them better and listened.

"Marian Aborn said, 'What did you lock her in for—she doesn't know anything!' and my guardian replied, 'Not yet, but she's a smart kid. See if you can gain her confidence and get hold of the jewels.' "

As Laura paused, a terrible thought came to Nancy. Were the Aborns *thieves?* But they could not be, she argued, if Marie Pendleton had trusted the couple to take care of her daughter. "And besides, I gather the Donnells think they are nice people." Aloud she asked, "What happened next?"

"I thought I must have heard them wrong," the auburn-haired girl said slowly, "but I suddenly remembered Mother telling me always to take good care of her jewelry. So I took it from my handbag and hid it underneath the mattress of the bed.

"Just as I finished doing this, the door to my room opened. Mrs. Aborn stood there, looking very friendly. She offered to help unpack my bags, and admired several dresses as I hung them in the closet—"

"And then—" Nancy pressed.

Laura said that she and Mrs. Aborn had prepared a tasty dinner, then she and the couple had watched television for a while.

"Just before we went upstairs to bed, Mrs. Aborn said it would be a good idea for me to put my mother's jewels in the wall safe in the living room. I agreed and said that I would give them to her in the morning."

"What was Mrs. Aborn's reaction to this?" Hannah asked.

"Oh, both she and her husband became very angry. They said that apparently I didn't trust them to take care of a few insignificant gems, while they in turn had the responsibility of caring for a penniless orphan! Oh, Nancy, I thought Mother had a lot of money! Mrs. Aborn yelled at me and said I was ungrateful and a big burden to them. They were sorry they had ever agreed to take me!

"I can't explain how I felt," Laura went on, her

hands shaking with nervousness. "I was just numb. Then I burst into tears and rushed to my room."

Laura said that finally she had fallen asleep and awakened this morning to find she was again locked in.

"At eight o'clock Mrs. Aborn opened the door, acting very friendly, and said breakfast was ready in the kitchen."

"Was anything said about last night?" Nancy asked.

Laura said no, that the Aborns had acted as though nothing had happened. "But a strange thing occurred after breakfast," Laura stated. "Mr. Aborn took a small package from the refrigerator and left the house, saying he would be back later. Before he went he said I would be sorry if I didn't co-operate with them!"

"I presume he meant to hand over the jewels," Hannah guessed, and Laura nodded.

"I knew then that I had to leave their house and also get word to Nancy. While Mrs. Aborn was emptying the rubbish I tried to use the phone, but she caught me and twisted my arm, then hung up the receiver!"

"You see, I was right, Hannah!" Nancy exclaimed, and told Laura her theory about the call.

"Were you locked up again?" Hannah asked.

Laura explained that before Mrs. Aborn could do this she had run past her and barricaded herself inside the bedroom, not wanting the jewels to be unguarded. At that moment the doorbell had rung. Apparently Mrs. Aborn had not answered it, for the woman had kept quiet for a long while on the first floor.

"So I quickly took my handbag and the jewels, and climbed down a trellis outside my window," Laura said. "Once I was on the detour I was lucky enough to get a ride to the highway and there I caught a bus to River Heights. I took a taxi to your house."

As Laura sat back with an exhausted sigh, Hannah stood up. "You're worn out, dear," the housekeeper said. "I'm going to get you a cup of hot tea and you're not to say another word until you've drunk it!"

With that, she bustled out of the room and returned shortly with a small tray on which was a cup of hot tea and a piece of toast. By the time Laura had finished the snack, color had returned to her cheeks and she looked more relaxed.

"I wonder if we should report your experience to the police," Nancy mused.

"What could we tell them?" Laura quavered.

"That's the point," Nancy continued. "We could tell them that the Aborns tried to get your jewels, but of course they would deny it all. It would be their word against yours."

"And I don't have definite proof!" Laura said dejectedly.

Nancy patted the girl's hand. "We'll do everything we can to help you, Laura. You've really had a terrible experience, you poor girl."

"Nancy, you're a real friend," Laura said. Tears came into her eyes. "Mr. Aborn is my legal guardian—I saw the papers—but what am I going to do?"

"You'll stay with us," Hannah said quickly, "and when Mr. Drew comes home he'll know how to handle the situation."

Nancy was quiet, but she was doing a lot of figuring. Something mysterious was going on at Melrose Lake. She intended to find out for herself what it was.

CHAPTER IX

A Valuable Inheritance

IF IT had been possible Nancy would have started out for Melrose Lake at once, but she felt that Laura needed her. Besides, there was a job to do for her father at the Browns' barbecue next day.

"Helping Dad comes first," Nancy decided.

Laura spoke again of her mother's affairs. "She used to say I'd always be financially independent if anything happened to her."

"We'll find out," Nancy said, and then took Laura upstairs so she might shower and rest.

In the meantime, Nancy selected some of her own clothes for the visitor. When she appeared at the dinner table, Hannah declared that Laura looked pretty as a picture and much more relaxed.

"I am—thanks to both of you," their guest said gratefully.

When the meal was finished the two girls sat out on the Drews' porch. To cheer up her guest, Nancy told Laura of her funny experience with the French poodles, while trying to get volunteers for the youth center. The young detective did not mention her real reason for calling at the apartment.

Laura giggled. "I wish I could have been with you," she said. "Tell me, Nancy, have you any souvenirs of the mysteries you've solved?"

"Two trophies." Nancy displayed a mantel clock and a valuable silver urn. Laughingly she told Laura that her father often said she would have the house cluttered before she finished her career!

Just then the telephone rang and Hannah called from upstairs that Mr. Drew was on the line. Nancy hurried to talk with him.

"Nancy, I've come across some evidence that indicates Mr. Hamilton, or some person working for him in the trust department, was behind the security thefts. A detective is tailing Hamilton, and if he tries to leave town, the Monroe police will be notified."

"How about the others in his department?" Nancy asked.

"They're being watched, too, but not so steadily. Of course we don't want to arrest an innocent man."

Nancy said she hoped the guilty person would make a misstep soon so the case might be solved, and told her father what she had learned of the River Heights suspects since she had seen him.

He suggested that she keep trying to contact the Dowds. "And that reminds me," the lawyer said. "You can forget about Mr. Herbert Brown being suspicious." He explained that Brown was a personal friend of the bank president's and had been cleared.

Nancy was relieved to hear this. "I'll keep trying to get in touch with the Dowds," she promised.

Next, she told her father about Laura Pendleton's flight from the Aborns' home. "Do you think we should report her experience with them to the police?" she asked.

Mr. Drew said no, that so far the two girls had only their suspicions of the couple's dishonesty, even though Laura had overheard them talking about her jewels. "You need some concrete evidence before calling in the authorities," he stated.

"I thought I'd run up to Melrose Lake and do some sleuthing," she said.

"All right, but keep out of danger," he warned. "I'll be eager to hear what you find out. We'll have a conference when I get home and decide what we can do for Laura."

"Thanks, Dad." A moment later they bade each other good night and hung up.

As the teen-aged detective started for the porch, she had an inspiration. It was not essential now for her to meet Herbert Brown. If Don Cameron would agree to take Laura as a substitute to the barbecue party, it would leave Nancy free to go to Melrose Lake the next day!

"I'll ask Don if he'd mind. If he does—well, that's that."

Hopefully Nancy dialed the Cameron house. Don answered and the girl detective told him the problem.

"Wow! A real mystery!" he remarked. "If I didn't know what sleuthing means to you, Nancy, I'd say you were just trying to brush me off. But you have me feeling sorry for this Laura Pendleton, too. Okay. If she's willing to go with me, I'll be glad to take her. But I'm sure sorry you can't make it. See you another time."

"Thanks, Don. I shan't forget this. Of course if Laura won't go, I'll keep the date. 'By now."

As Nancy walked toward the porch, she smilingly crossed her fingers, hoping that Laura would agree to the plan. Stepping outside, Nancy asked, "How would you like to go to a barbecue tomorrow, Laura?"

The girl's face glowed with anticipation. "It would be fun!" she exclaimed. "Where, Nancy?"

When the plan was explained, Laura said, "Oh, but I don't want to take your date away from you."

"Don and I have already arranged everything," Nancy assured her. Then she told of her desire to do some sleuthing at Melrose Lake.

At once Laura said she was afraid to have Nancy go to the Aborns' home. "There's no telling what my guardian might do to you," she said fearfully. "He has a terrible temper, and if he learns you're helping me—"

"He won't learn that," Nancy said determinedly.

Reluctantly Laura agreed to Nancy's whole scheme. "But if anything should happen to you, I— I'd just want to die!" she declared.

Before the girls went to bed, Hannah suggested that Laura's jewelry be put into the wall safe in Mr. Drew's study.

"Dad, Hannah, and I are the only persons who know the combination," Nancy told Laura.

"It would be a good idea," the brown-eyed girl replied. "First, I'd like to show you some of Mother's treasures. She gave them to me before her last illness."

"Do you have this in writing?" Hannah asked.

"Yes, I do. Why?"

"Then the jewelry wouldn't be part of your

mother's estate," Mrs. Gruen answered, "and there'd be no tax on it."

Laura took a package from her handbag and opened it. She displayed a string of priceless matched pearls, a gorgeous diamond clip and earrings, several jeweled pins set with rubies, pearls, and emeralds, and six rings, including one with a brilliant star sapphire.

Nancy and Hannah were astounded. "Why, this is the most beautiful collection I've ever seen!" Nancy exclaimed. She pointed to a ring set with a perfect aquamarine. "I love this!"

Laura smiled. "That was Mother's favorite," she said. "My father gave it to her on their first wedding anniversary."

"Thank goodness your guardian didn't find these things!" Hannah declared.

Finally the jewels were put into the safe and everyone went to bed.

Nancy awoke at seven o'clock the next morning. After taking a shower, she decided to wear a forest-green cotton dress and flat-heeled brown play shoes.

Laura was still sleeping when Nancy joined Mrs. Gruen at breakfast. The housekeeper was using a cane.

"My ankle feels almost as good as new," Hannah announced. "I've discarded the crutches."

Nancy was delighted to hear this. As they ate, she and the housekeeper talked about the young sleuth's trip.

"I'll worry about you every second until you return home," Mrs. Gruen declared. "If you're not here by ten thirty, I'll notify the police."

Nancy grinned. "I'll try to be here by suppertime. If not, I'll call you."

A short while later Nancy battled the early-morning traffic through the city. Reaching the outskirts, she took the road to Melrose Lake.

"Poor Laura," she thought, wondering what the day would disclose about the girl's strange guardian and his wife.

If Laura were really penniless, maybe the man thought he had a legitimate right to take and sell the jewelry for the girl's support. But his wife had bragged about having plenty of money to take care of their ward.

After a time Nancy came to the Melrose Lake detour. Laura had told her there was a sign marked "Eagle Rock" in front of the lane leading to her guardian's property.

Presently Nancy approached the spot where the pine tree had fallen. Fortunately, it had been removed.

She drove more slowly, afraid of inadvertently missing the Eagle Rock sign. Then, sighting the turnoff, Nancy left the detour.

"This ring was Mother's favorite," Laura said

She had gone but a few hundred feet along the Aborns' road when she decided it might be safer to walk. After parking along the side of the roadway, she started off. In a few minutes Nancy suddenly caught sight of a man walking rapidly through the woods. He carried a small bundle under his arm.

"Jacob Aborn!" she thought, recognizing his profile and the peculiar stoop of his shoulders.

Nancy recalled Laura's story of her guardian taking a small package from the refrigerator and leaving the house with it. What was in the bundle and where was he taking it?

"I'm going to find out!" Nancy declared. Without hesitation, she quietly plunged into the thicket. Following at a safe distance she managed to keep the man in sight.

"He doesn't seem to be worried about being followed," Nancy thought. "He must not have heard my car when I turned into the lane." She continued her musing. "I'm glad I wore this green dress. It's good camouflage!"

Just then a twig crackled under her foot, breaking the stillness of the woods. Jacob Aborn turned and looked back, frowning. He stood a minute, listening intently. Only by ducking quickly behind a large bush had Nancy avoided detection.

"I'd better be more careful if I don't want to get caught," she warned herself.

As the man continued through the forest Nancy followed, painstakingly avoiding twigs or loose stones. She kept well behind him.

"Wouldn't it be a joke on me if he's just a bird watcher!" She giggled at the thought. "And maybe that package has his lunch in it!"

Laughing to herself, Nancy picked her way through the woods as she trailed Laura Pendleton's guardian. Suddenly he disappeared behind a clump of high blueberry bushes. Nancy hurried forward. When she reached the spot the girl detective looked about in all directions.

"Which way did he go?" she asked herself.

Jacob Aborn seemed to have vanished into thin air!

CHAPTER X

The Danger Sign

ALERT for possible danger, Nancy moved forward with the utmost caution. It occurred to her that possibly Aborn had become aware he was being followed and had hidden in the bushes to watch the pursuer.

"I'll walk into a trap!" Nancy thought with alarm. "Mr. Aborn will learn I'm spying on him and everything will be ruined!"

With great caution she moved from one bush and tree to another. Laura's guardian was not hiding behind any of them.

"That's funny," Nancy said to herself.

She examined the ground, almost expecting there would be a cave or secret tunnel in the vicinity. But the earth was firm and in many places very rocky.

Finally Nancy came to a tiny clearing. On the far side attached to a large oak was a crudely printed wooden sign which read:

PRIVATE PROPERTY. KEEP OUT. DANGER!

"I wonder if that's where Mr. Aborn went and why?" the young detective asked herself.

She waited several minutes, then decided to cross the clearing. She was not stopped. Entering the woods again, she saw a dilapidated shack. The windows had been boarded up, and the roof sagged.

"One good gust of wind would blow the place over," Nancy said to herself.

She stepped from among the bushes and stood in the shadow of the trees, curiously surveying the building. Was it possible that Jacob Aborn had entered it?

Nancy's eyes searched the ground for footprints. Directly ahead, in the soft earth, she saw the fresh mark of a man's shoe. Instantly her suspicions were confirmed.

Jacob Aborn had come this way!

"I'll just have a look at this shack," the young sleuth decided.

After quickly glancing about to make certain she was not being watched, Nancy hurried forward. Tiptoeing across the front porch, she quietly tried the door. It was locked. Nancy walked around to the rear door and found that it likewise was securely fastened.

Although disappointed, Nancy was unwilling to give up. Making a complete circuit of the shack, she saw a window from which several boards had fallen. It was too high for her to peer through. Nancy returned to the rear of the building to get an old box that she had seen. She set it beneath the window and mounted it.

Pressing her face against the glass, she gazed inside. The room, apparently a kitchen, was bare of furniture and covered with dust and cobwebs.

"I wish I could get inside," Nancy thought.

She was about to climb down from the box when a strange feeling came over her. Though she had heard no sound, Nancy sensed that unfriendly eyes were watching her every move.

Before she could turn around and look over her shoulder, a coarse, angry voice barked into her ear:

"What are you doing here, young lady?"

Nancy wheeled and faced Jacob Aborn!

With as much dignity as she could muster, the girl detective stepped to the ground and regarded the man with composure. His eyes burned with rage.

"I was merely curious," Nancy replied. "And may I ask why *you* are here?"

"Yes, I'll tell you. I'm looking for my ward."

"You mean Laura Pendleton?"

"Yes. Who else? I thought maybe she was hiding here. But nobody's in the shack."

"Why in the world would Laura hide in this ramshackle place?" Nancy asked, trying to show as much surprise as possible.

"Search me," Mr. Aborn said, then added angrily, his eyes boring Nancy's, "Laura has run away!"

"*Run away?*" Nancy repeated.

"Yes. Yesterday. I'll tell you something about that ward of mine—" A crafty light came into Jacob Aborn's eyes as he went on, "At times she acts unbalanced—thinks folks don't treat her right."

"Indeed?" said Nancy, pretending to be shocked.

By now Laura's guardian had calmed down. When he spoke again he was once more the pleasant man Nancy had met at the Montewago Hotel.

"It's for Laura's own good that she ought to return home," he said. "Mrs. Aborn is dreadfully upset. She loves Laura just like a mother. Miss Drew, have you heard from Laura by any chance?"

Nancy was on her guard. "Why should I hear from her?" she countered. "We never met until that accident on the lake and she came to rescue my friend Helen and me."

Mr. Aborn did not pursue the subject. Instead, he said, "Laura's a nervous, high-strung girl. Why, do you know she locked herself in her room the entire time she was with us—wouldn't eat, or even let us try to help her?"

"Terrible!" Nancy said, pretending to be shocked. "Laura does need help."

Secretly Nancy felt that Jacob Aborn was telling this version of the locked-door story to cover his own actions, in case they came to light.

"Have you notified the police, Mr. Aborn?" she asked, probing for further information.

"We have a private detective working on the matter," the man stated. "We don't want any bad publicity because of dear Marie Pendleton's memory. She entrusted Laura to my care because she knew how much my wife and I would love the girl."

Nancy suddenly was finding it hard to concentrate on what Mr. Aborn was saying. Was she wrong or had she heard a sound inside the shack?

"This is very strange," she told herself. "But I don't dare pursue the subject or Mr. Aborn will really become suspicious." Aloud she said, "I certainly hope Laura is all right. Well, I must go now. I have some friends here at Melrose Lake I plan to call on." She paused, then added lightly, "In fact, I believe you know them, Mr. Aborn— the Donnell family."

The man looked startled, then recovered himself. "Oh, yes. Fine family. Say hello to them for me, please."

Nancy promised that she would. Since Mr. Aborn made no move to accompany her, she said good-by and walked rapidly back to the spot where her convertible was parked.

As Nancy climbed into it, she cast a glance over her shoulder. There was no sign of Mr. Aborn. Had he gone into the shack? Was someone there? Had he been delivering packages to the person?

Nancy started the car's motor and backed out to the main road. As she drove along, her thoughts were entirely on Mr. Aborn. She had no doubt but that the man had been lying about Laura's behavior.

"I must find out more about that man," Nancy decided.

Reaching the highway, she stopped at a service station, had the gas tank of her car filled, and asked directions to the Donnell home. The attendant told her how to reach the place, and a short while later Nancy drew up before a lovely redwood house located well off the road.

She got out and rang the front doorbell. There was no answer. Nancy walked around to the back of the house. A gardener was there, trimming the flower beds.

"Howdy, miss!" the elderly man hailed her. "Looking for the Donnells?"

"Yes. Are they away?" Nancy inquired.

"Yep. They're visiting relatives in Crescent Gardens 'til tonight. Any message?"

Nancy said no, that she would call again, and thanked the man. As she drove away Nancy was disappointed that she had been unable to pick up any information regarding Mr. Aborn.

"I don't want to leave Melrose Lake until I have learned *something* to help Laura," she thought. "Mr. Aborn may trace her whereabouts to our home and force Laura to return with him before Dad gets back to town. I suppose he has a legal right to do it."

At last an idea came to Nancy. "I'll go to one of the hotels on the lake and engage a room. Then, after it gets dark, I'll do a little more investigating."

Fortunately, Nancy always carried an overnight case in her car trunk. It contained pajamas and robe, two changes of clothing, toilet articles, and, this time of year, a bathing suit.

Presently she saw a large white building ahead of her. Its green lawn sloped down to the sandy beach. On the stone pillar at the side of the driveway was the sign: *Beach Cliff Hotel*.

"I think I'll stop here," Nancy decided. She parked her car and entered the pleasant lobby. In a few minutes she had registered and been taken to a comfortable room overlooking the lake.

"I'll telephone home," Nancy said to herself, "and tell Hannah where I am."

As Nancy placed the call, a chilling thought suddenly popped into her mind. Perhaps the detective whom Aborn had engaged had already traced the runaway girl, and knew Nancy had not told all she knew about Laura. If so, Nancy might find that her guest had already been whisked away from the Drew home!

CHAPTER XI

Trapped!

WHEN Hannah Gruen answered the telephone at the Drew residence, Nancy at once asked, "Is Laura all right?"

"Why, of course," Hannah answered in surprise. "She's upstairs setting her hair for the party this afternoon."

"Well, tell her to be very careful," Nancy urged. "Mr. Aborn has a detective looking for her!"

"Oh dear!" exclaimed Mrs. Gruen. "And when will you be home, Nancy?"

The young detective explained where she was and that she planned to stay at Melrose Lake and do more sleuthing.

"I think I may be on the trail of something big."

"I don't like the idea of you prowling around the Aborns' home in the dead of night," the housekeeper objected.

"I'll be careful," Nancy promised. "I may even get home tonight."

"Well, all right," Hannah consented reluctantly. "By the way, Nancy, I had a repairman fix the window in Mr. Drew's study this morning, and also requested the police to keep a lookout for anything suspicious going on in this neighborhood."

"Wonderful!" Nancy said, feeling relieved. "Any more news?"

"Everything's quiet here," Hannah reported. "And Laura seems happy."

Laura came to speak to Nancy and was alarmed when she heard that a detective was looking for her. "But I won't go back to those awful Aborns! They can't make me! If they try it, I'll—I'll run right to the police!"

"That's a good idea," said Nancy. "By the way, I'd like to do some sleuthing at the Aborn house. I may want to get inside without ringing the bell." The young sleuth chuckled. "Since it's now your house too, may I have permission to go in and look around?"

"You certainly may," said Laura with a giggle. "If no doors are unlocked, try my bedroom window. I left it open a crack and there's a sturdy rose trellis right alongside it."

"Terrific!" said Nancy elatedly.

After she completed the call, Nancy went to

the hotel coffee shop for a hearty lunch. Since it was now almost one thirty, the room was empty.

After eating, Nancy put on her bathing suit and wandered down to the beach. A boy in attendance gave her a towel and Nancy stretched out on the sand, unaware of the steadfast glance of a couple hidden behind a large green-and-white striped umbrella not far away. They nodded to each other, then when Nancy was not looking, they quickly left the beach.

"Guess we're safe," the woman muttered. "She's here to stay and have a good time."

As the strong rays of the sun beat down on the unsuspecting girl, she rehearsed her plan for the evening. When it was dark she would visit both Jacob Aborn's home and also the shack in the woods, if time permitted.

"I'll miss Dad's call tonight," Nancy reflected.

Standing up half an hour later, Nancy put on her bathing cap and walked to the water. She stuck her toe in. The lake water felt icy cold, and Nancy noticed that there were more people on the beach than in swimming. Nevertheless, she waded out to where it was deep enough to make a surface dive and plunged in. Once she was wet, the water was invigorating.

After swimming for a while, Nancy came back to her beach towel and dried off. Then she returned to her room, showered, and slept for two hours, realizing that the rest would give her more endurance for the evening ahead.

Awakening at six o'clock, Nancy put on the simple black cotton dress from her suitcase and pumps. After brushing her hair until it snapped with electricity, she was ready for supper.

"What will it be this evening, miss?" asked the friendly waitress.

Nancy selected steak, a baked potato, and tossed salad, then sat back to enjoy the soft dinner music playing in the background. The orchestra was in an adjoining lounge.

Nearby diners regarded the lone girl with interest, for the prospect of the daring adventure had brought a becoming flush to her cheeks.

"If I'm wrong in suspecting Jacob Aborn of being dishonest," thought Nancy, "then I guess I'd better give up sleuthing!"

Upon leaving the dining room an hour later, she lingered on the porch for a few minutes, watching couples dance. As a red-haired young man began to walk toward Nancy with an invitation in his eyes for her to dance, she hastily went to her room.

Chuckling to herself, Nancy said aloud, "Romance and detective work won't mix tonight!" Then she changed to walking shoes, sweater, and skirt.

The moment it became dark enough for her

purpose, Nancy left the hotel in her car. As she drew near the Aborns' lane a short while later, she turned the convertible off the road and ran it into a clump of bushes where it would not be seen.

Switching off the engine and locking the doors, Nancy started down the lane leading to the house, holding her flashlight securely. She found the windows of the house dark.

"The Aborns are out, I guess," she told herself. "Well, that means I can do some looking around."

Circling the structure cautiously, Nancy noted that the second-floor wing, where the bedrooms apparently were located, was in the back. She found the trellis easily.

"I'll try the doors first," Nancy decided, and darted to the front. Gently turning the handle, she found the door locked.

An investigation of two other doors revealed that they, too, were securely fastened.

"I guess I'll have to climb after all," Nancy said to herself.

As quietly as possible, she climbed the trellis. It wobbled and creaked a little but did not give way. When Nancy reached the window ledge of Laura's bedroom, she found to her delight that the window raised easily. She crawled through and switched on her flashlight.

As Nancy tiptoed across the room, which was in

disorder, she heard a noise. Halting, she listened. A car was approaching the house. Looking out the window she could barely make out the figures of a man and a woman who alighted. Who were they and what should Nancy do?

"I'll stay right here," she determined.

As Nancy waited tensely she realized someone was walking up the stairs. Quickly Nancy closed the window without a sound. As she looked around for a hiding place she saw a closet, and darted inside it, switching off her flashlight. Crouched in a far corner behind some of Laura's dresses, Nancy scarcely dared to breathe.

The door to the room was opened a moment later and the boudoir lamps switched on. Cautiously Nancy peered out through the keyhole in the closet door. She saw Jacob Aborn!

The man went directly to Laura's dressing table. Apparently he had not heard Nancy, for he did not glance toward the closet.

Ruthlessly he jerked out drawers from the dressing table and emptied their contents upon the bed. As he surveyed the assortment of tiny bottles, boxes, and other paraphernalia, Laura's guardian gave a disgusted grunt.

"Last place to look!" he said, as if addressing someone out in the hall, probably his wife. "Guess Laura really took the jewels with her. Well, I'll soon have them back!"

Nancy's heart leaped. There was no longer any doubt in her mind as to the character of this man. She was now certain that his sole interest in Laura was to get possession of her property! Only the girl's opportune escape from the house had prevented him from seizing the valuable jewelry collection!

"Laura's mother couldn't have known his true character, or she wouldn't have entrusted her daughter to Aborn's care," Nancy pondered.

Her thoughts came to an abrupt end as the man moved toward the closet. Fearfully, Nancy ducked down behind Laura's dresses again and fervently hoped that she would not be discovered.

Suddenly, as Nancy's legs began to grow cramped, the closet door was jerked violently open. Jacob Aborn looked in!

CHAPTER XII

A Black Abyss

As JACOB ABORN stared into the closet where Nancy was hiding, the girl detective wished wildly that she were invisible. There was no telling what harm the man might inflict if he saw her!

"He has such a violent temper," Nancy realized.

But Aborn's glance did not stray to the dress section. Instead, he reached up for two large suitcases which were on a shelf above the clothes. He set them on the floor outside and shut the closet door.

Beads of perspiration trickled down Nancy's neck as she relaxed. Presently she heard the man leave the room and shut the hall door with a loud bang.

Nancy waited a moment, then left her hiding

place. "I suppose I'd better leave while I can," she advised herself.

But running away from a chance to pick up a clue was not in Nancy's nature. As she heard Laura's guardian descending the stairs to the first floor, she became aware of a woman's voice somewhere below. Nancy decided, "I'll stay and see what's going on."

Before leaving Laura's bedroom she gave it a final searching look and shook her head, puzzled. The room was one which Nancy would be happy to call her own. The feminine furnishings and good colonial pieces showed evidence of discerning taste. They did not fit the Aborns' character. Perhaps an interior decorator had planned it!

"One could believe from this room that the Aborns really wanted Laura," Nancy pondered.

It just did not make sense. Many criminals, Nancy knew, laid the groundwork to lull any suspicion on the part of their victim, then cornered him. But Laura had not even been settled in her new home when the Aborns had begun to persecute her.

Soundlessly Nancy opened the bedroom door, and keeping her flashlight low to the floor, tiptoed along the carpeted hall. Step by step, she edged down the stairway to the floor below. Here there was no sign of activity but Nancy saw a light shining through louvered doors to her left.

"That's probably the kitchen. The Aborns are in there," she thought.

A moment later the woman said, "Here's the combination. I'll pack this stuff while you open the safe."

Quickly Nancy stole into the living room and hastily ducked out of sight behind a large sofa. She was just in time. One of the louvered doors opened and Laura's guardian came into the living room carrying a suitcase. He flicked on a table lamp.

Near it hung the small oil painting of a ship. Aborn lifted it from the wall and set the picture against a chair.

Nancy's eyes widened as she saw that the painting had concealed a wall safe. Aborn deftly twirled the dial to the left, then several notches to the right, and back to the left again. He swung the safe door open.

With a grunt of satisfaction, the man removed several packages of bank notes and some papers which looked like stock certificates. Mr. Aborn chortled and called to his wife:

"When we get the rest of these cashed, you and I will be set for life—thanks to Laura and a few others."

Nancy, startled, almost gave herself away. So Laura did have a sizable inheritance other than the jewelry! But how had the securities reached the safe? Had Aborn brought them here or was he stealing them from someone else? Nancy felt more confused by the moment.

As her thoughts raced, Aborn replaced the loose papers in the safe and closed it. Then he put the money and securities into the suitcase. Giving a tired yawn, he switched off the lamp and left the room.

"Guess I'll turn in," he called to his wife. "Got to be up early tomorrow and get Fred. You ready?"

"Yes."

Marian Aborn came from the kitchen carrying the other bag. Together the couple ascended the stairs. Nancy heard a bedroom door above close.

"Now I must get the police," the girl detective thought.

She paused for several seconds, after coming from behind the couch, to stretch her cramped limbs. "I'd better go out the front door," she decided. "The bedrooms don't overlook that."

Noiselessly Nancy slipped outside and started for her hidden car. Then a temptation came to her. "Why don't I investigate that shack in the woods first? I may have an even bigger story to tell the police! I'll do it!"

Taking a deep breath of air, Nancy hurried toward the path leading to the dilapidated building. Had she been right about having heard some-

one inside? Was he a friend or an enemy of
Aborn's? Were the packages being carried there
and what did they contain? Loot?

"Maybe just food," Nancy concluded. "But being taken to whom?"

Beaming her flashlight on the ground, the
young detective soon picked up the trail she had
taken earlier in the day. It was quiet and eerie as
she stumbled along the uneven ground. Nancy became apprehensive once or twice as she heard
scuffling noises of forest creatures in the under-
brush, but went on.

"I wish Dad were here now," she thought fervently.

Nancy reached the shack without mishap and
paused in front of it. A sixth sense seemed to tell
her there was someone inside who needed help.
No person would stay in such a place unless
forced to.

"This is no time for me to hesitate," she told
herself.

As Nancy moved toward the rear of the tumble-
down building, she glanced at her flashlight and
was alarmed to see that it was beginning to grow
dim.

"Just my luck when I need it the most!"

In an attempt to save the battery, Nancy
switched off the light. As her eyes became accus-
tomed to the darkness, she moved toward the

window she had looked through earlier that day. Appraising it, the young sleuth realized that the window ledge was too high from the ground for her to climb through unassisted, even when standing on the box.

Undaunted, she began to examine the other windows. On the south side of the shack she found one which opened from the rickety porch. It was boarded up.

"This is my entry," Nancy determined.

She began searching the yard for something with which to pry off the boards, and finally found a stout stick. Nancy began wedging it between the boards with all her might.

The first board offered stubborn resistance. Then, with a groan and a squeak, it gave way. The remaining boards were removed with less difficulty.

To Nancy's joy, the window was unlocked! Pushing it up, she beamed her flashlight inside. The room beyond was bare and quiet as a tomb.

"Well, here comes Nancy Drew, housebreaker and spy!" Nancy thought with amused determination. "It's certain now no one lives here."

When she was halfway through the window the young sleuth hesitated without knowing just why. She glanced back over her shoulder. A queer sensation made Nancy quiver as she turned searching eyes toward the woods.

"How silly!" she scolded herself. "No one's there. It's just nerves."

Bravely Nancy swung herself through the window. Hastily she moved toward an adjoining room, noting that her flashlight was growing dimmer. Soon she would be left in total darkness! She must hurry!

Her light revealed a small room, also empty, its walls and floor dusty from long lack of any occupant's care. Nancy was disappointed to find nothing of interest.

"I'd better leave and drive to police headquarters," she thought.

Just then Nancy's flashlight revealed a trap door in the floor. Quickly she moved over toward it. But she had taken only a few steps when an unusual sound arrested her attention. Had she heard a board creak behind her, or was it a night sound from the woods?

After hesitating a second, Nancy again started for the trap door. As she reached down to grasp the ring in it, her body became tense.

This time there was no mistake. She had heard a peculiar sound which seemed to come from beneath the floor.

"It sounded like a groan!" Nancy decided. She felt cold all over.

Someone was imprisoned in the cellar! Who? And why?

As Nancy tugged at the ring, another idea came to her. This might be a trap laid for her!

"Oh, what should I do?" she thought, hesitating. There was still time to run away from danger.

But the fear that some person was in distress gave her the courage to open the trap door. As it swung upward, Nancy saw before her a flight of stone steps, leading down into complete darkness. A gust of damp, musty air struck her in the face and momentarily repulsed her.

Nancy glanced nervously at her flashlight. The battery could not last much longer. Already the light was so weak that she could barely see the steps in front of her. Did she dare investigate the cellar?

"It won't take long," she thought.

She descended the steps and came to a landing. The rest of the stairway went toward the left. Nancy peered anxiously into the black abyss below.

To her horror, she saw a man stretched out full length on a bench. His face was turned upward and Nancy caught a full glimpse of the countenance.

He was Jacob Aborn!

CHAPTER XIII

An Actor's Ruse

SPELLBOUND, Nancy stood like a stone image, gazing down into the face of Jacob Aborn. How had the man reached the bungalow ahead of her? What was he doing sleeping in the musty cellar of the old shack?

As these thoughts flashed through Nancy's mind, the beam of her flashlight flickered again. Then it went out, leaving her in total darkness.

Sheer panic took possession of the girl detective. Something very strange was going on! She must not be caught in a trap!

Turning, she gave a low cry and stumbled up the stairway and toward the window through which she had entered. Her flight was abruptly checked as she banged one foot on something metallic that moved ahead of her. In a second she smelled kerosene.

"A lantern!" she decided.

The thought of a light gave her hope. She felt around and discovered an old-time oil lantern.

Collecting her wits, she stopped and listened for any sounds of pursuit. There were none. The shack appeared as deserted and silent as before.

"I'm sure that was Jacob Aborn down in the cellar," Nancy thought in perplexity. "I didn't imagine it. But how did he get here so fast? After I left his house I didn't waste much time."

Suddenly an amazing thought came to Nancy. Was the man she had seen by chance a brother, even a twin, of Jacob Aborn? He might be honest and Jacob had found him in the way!

"I'm going to find out!" Nancy declared excitedly.

Eagerly she reached into the pocket of her dress, recalling that at dinner she had taken a pack of matches from the hotel dining table for her souvenir collection. Good! The pack was still there!

Striking a match she was pleased to discover that the lantern was half full of oil. Someone had used it recently, for the glass was clean. Nancy lighted the wick and a flame spurted up. Carrying the lantern, she returned to the trap door.

Suddenly, from below, Nancy heard a moan of pain. This was followed by a pitiful cry of "Help!"

"That settles it," the worried girl thought.

As she descended the steps, the lantern's flick-

From below came a pitiful cry of "Help!"

ering glow revealed that the cellar was dungeon-like, with solid stone walls and no windows.

She held the light high above the figure on the bench. A man, deathly pale, was lying where she had first seen him.

But he was not Laura's guardian!

"There's certainly a startling resemblance, though," Nancy thought, her heart filled with pity for this unfortunate stranger.

Dropping to her knees, she felt his pulse. It was faint but regular.

"He's just unconscious," she told herself in relief.

At the same time, Nancy saw with horror a large chain around the man's waist. It was attached to the prisoner in such a way that it allowed him some freedom of motion and yet held him captive. Was Jacob Aborn responsible for this atrocity? Nancy wondered angrily.

"I must do something to revive this man," she decided, "and get him away from here."

Picking up the lantern, Nancy mounted the cellar steps two at a time. She headed for a small sink in one corner of the room above, where she had seen a pump.

After a search through the cupboard she at last found a battered tin cup. Quickly pumping water into it, she returned to the cellar.

Nancy wet her handkerchief and applied it

gently to the prisoner's forehead. Then she sprin-
kled a little of the water on his face and chafed his
wrists. The man stirred slightly and moaned.

As she gazed anxiously into his face, Nancy wondered how she could have mistaken him for Jacob
Aborn. Although the two men were of the same
age, and had similar facial characteristics, the
prisoner was gaunt and thin. His features, con-
trary to Mr. Aborn's, were gentle and relaxed.

Now Nancy saw that the man was slowly regaining consciousness. As his eyes fluttered open he
cried "Help!" feebly, then stared into Nancy's
face, amazed.

"Help has come," Nancy said quietly.

The man attempted to raise himself to a sitting
position with Nancy's aid. "Didn't—think—help
—would—ever come," he murmured. Then he
saw the cup in Nancy's hand and asked for water.

Nancy steadied the cup while he drank. Finally
the man leaned against the wall. "First water I've
had in twenty-four hours," he said more clearly.

The young sleuth was horrified. She introduced
herself, then asked, "Who are you—and who did
this terrible thing to you?"

A bitter expression passed over the prisoner's
face. "I'm Jacob Aborn," he said. "A crook by the
name of Stumpy Dowd took over my house, imprisoned me here, and somehow or other arranged
for my new ward, Laura Pendleton, to come to my

home earlier than she was expected. Yesterday he told me that he had the girl's inheritance in his possession—and showed bonds to prove it."

"You're Jacob Aborn!" Nancy repeated, as the prisoner, exhausted by these words, leaned against the wall.

Quickly Nancy's mind flashed back to everything that had happened since she had met Laura. The puzzling questions that had bothered her about the girl's guardian now became clear. Most of all, it was a relief to know that the person to whom Marie Pendleton had entrusted her daughter's care was not a criminal.

Equally important, Nancy realized that Stephen Dowd—alias Stumpy—used his talent as an actor and skill with make-up to fool other people, and then probably swindled them. The young sleuth wondered if there was a tie-in between Laura's inheritance and the Monroe National Bank thefts of stocks and bonds. She must find out from Jacob Aborn, but the police should be notified immediately, as well as her father.

Aloud Nancy said, "I want to hear the whole story of what has happened to you, Mr. Aborn, but first—"

Briefly, she told of having met the man who had impersonated him and of seeing Laura at Twin Lakes. Nancy was about to add that Laura was now at her home when Mr. Aborn said:

"If Stumpy caught you here once today we'd better get out right now!" He told Nancy that Dowd kept the key to the padlock on his chains on a hook near the stairway.

"This is a lucky break," said Nancy. She snatched the lantern from the floor and started toward the stairs.

"Please hurry," Mr. Aborn said faintly. "Stumpy Dowd is a dangerous criminal! He boasted to me that he and his accomplices have victimized several people besides Laura!"

Nancy anxiously moved the lantern up and down, illuminating the dingy walls. Just above her head to the left she finally saw the hook, with a key dangling from it.

"I have it!" she exclaimed triumphantly.

As Nancy hurried back to Mr. Aborn's side she speculated on how the Dowds had found out about Mr. Aborn, his wife, and Laura.

"I'll have you free in a minute, Mr. Aborn," Nancy said, as she stooped over the bench.

While she worked on the rusty lock, Nancy asked if he had known the Dowds previously.

"Yes," he replied. "Mrs. Dowd was hired by my wife as a maid to come when we arrived. Soon after I reached the house her husband came. He grew quite loud and abusive and when I objected he knocked me unconscious. When I came to, I was chained in this cellar."

"How dreadful!" Nancy exclaimed. "But where is your wife?" she asked.

"She had to go to Florida unexpectedly. Her mother, who lives there, had an emergency operation. Marian went down to be with her and I moved into our new home." Mr. Aborn sighed. "Of course I haven't heard a word from her since I've been tied up here!"

"You'll be able to find out about her now," Nancy assured him. "Do you know how many people are working with Stumpy Dowd?"

"One or two others besides his wife, I believe. Stumpy Dowd is secretive about some things, although he boasted a lot. I did hear him mention the name Fred, but I don't know who he is."

When the padlock finally snapped open Nancy's spirits soared. Now the suitcase of securities that Stumpy Dowd had packed could be retrieved. The criminals could be apprehended and her father's case perhaps solved!

Meanwhile, neither Nancy nor Mr. Aborn had noticed a dark figure creeping slowly down the steps. Near and nearer the man came, a stout cane gripped tightly in his right hand.

"That's wonderful, Nancy!" Mr. Aborn exclaimed. "Now if I just knew where Laura is." As he spoke Mr. Aborn glanced up. A look of horror froze his face.

"Look out, Nancy!" he shouted.

CHAPTER XIV

A Desperate Situation

THE WARNING came too late. Before Nancy could turn, the end of the cane crashed down on her head. With a low moan of pain, she sagged to the floor and lay still.

How long she remained unconscious, the young sleuth did not know. When at last she opened her eyes Nancy found herself stretched out on the cold floor of the cellar. Bewildered, it was a full minute before she could account for the splitting pain in her head.

Then, with a shudder, the young sleuth remembered what had happened. She had been struck down from behind. Who was her assailant?

Nancy became aware that someone was standing over her, but objects whirled before her eyes and she could not distinguish the face. Then, gradually, her vision cleared. She saw Stumpy Dowd gazing down upon her, a satisfied leer on his face.

"Well, Miss Drew," he said mockingly, "we meet again. You've gotten in my way once too often!"

As Nancy started to speak, Dowd reached down. Catching Nancy by an arm, he jerked her roughly to her feet. Nancy was so weak that she nearly fell over.

Nevertheless, with a show of spirit, she said, "You'll regret this, I promise you!"

"Let the girl go," Jacob Aborn pleaded from the other side of the room. "Do anything you like to me, but set her free." Nancy saw that he was again padlocked.

Stumpy Dowd glared at his other prisoner. "It's quite impossible for me to release either of you," he said calmly. "You see, you both know too much."

Nancy was aware that resistance would be useless. Right now she did not have the strength to make a break for the stairs. But as the criminal began to unwind a long rope, Nancy realized that unless she thought of something the situation would be desperate. There would be no way to escape!

As Stumpy began to bind Nancy's feet together he said sarcastically, "Mr. Aborn will enjoy having company. And you two have so much to talk about."

An idea suddenly came to Nancy. She remembered that a detective who had called on her father a few months before had told her how it was possible to hold one's hands while being bound so as to slip the bonds later. He had given a demonstration.

"If I can only remember the correct position," Nancy prayed fervently.

When Dowd began to bind Nancy's wrists she tried to follow the detective's instructions. As the ropes cut into her flesh it seemed to Nancy that she must have made a mistake. Certainly there was little space between her wrists and the bonds.

"And now, just to make sure you won't get away—" Stumpy muttered with a sneer.

He took the end of the rope and ran it through a ring in the wall, knotting the rope fast.

"I guess that will hold you for a while and teach you not to meddle in affairs that are none of your business!" the man added.

Nancy Drew had never been so angry in her life, but she realized that any argument she might give would only provoke the man to further torture. So she set her jaw grimly and kept still.

"You'll pay for this, Dowd!" Jacob Aborn spoke up in a quavering voice. "When I get free—"

"When you get free!" Stumpy Dowd taunted.

"That's a laugh. Why, you fool, how do you propose to get help? If it hadn't been for this meddlesome Drew girl only the rats would have known you were here!"

Nancy could not help but remark quietly, "The police will catch you in the end."

"I doubt it," Dowd said with confidence. "I've covered my trail thoroughly. I've made plans to leave the country and I'd like to see the police or anyone else catch me!" He turned to Laura's guardian. "First, of course, we'll have to get the jewels away from Laura."

"How do you propose to do that," Nancy asked quickly, "when you don't know where she is?"

Stumpy Dowd laughed. "That's what you think. Laura is at your home in River Heights, Nancy Drew!"

As Nancy blinked, a look of horror came into Mr. Aborn's eyes. Nancy knew he was wondering why she had not mentioned Laura's being at her home. Also, he realized that his last hope of keeping Laura's whereabouts unknown was gone.

Nancy, too, was worried. What did Stumpy plan to do? Right now, he looked pleased at his prisoners' reactions.

"My wife overheard Laura placing a call to Nancy Drew in River Heights yesterday morning. When Laura ran away, we had a hunch she would go there. I asked my detective to find out."

Dowd said the sleuth had seen Laura leaving the house that afternoon with a young man. "I presume she left her jewels behind," he added. "But we'll get them before we leave this area!"

"Don't try anything foolish," Nancy warned.

"All my plans are well made," Dowd said coolly. "Too bad you aren't more cautious, Miss Drew."

He said that his wife had felt a draft in the house and gone downstairs to find the front door part way open. Then she had seen a girl heading into the woods and had awakened him. Dowd had figured out that it might be Nancy.

"That's the end of my story," he said, "except to tell you, Aborn, I sold your blue sedan this morning. The money helped pay for my new foreign car."

Jacob Aborn was so furious he almost choked. "You robber! You kidnaper!" he cried out.

"Tut, tut, none of that!" Dowd said. "You'll get your blood pressure up."

"Laura's not in your clutches, and she won't get there!" Aborn stormed. "And I can support her without any inheritance!"

Dowd shrugged. "It won't do any good to threaten me. You're my prisoner and don't forget it! After the jewels are mine—"

Nancy felt as if she would choke with rage. Mr. Aborn closed his eyes and seemed to have fainted.

Meanwhile, Stumpy Dowd had replaced the key on the wall—the hook supporting it, Nancy saw, was far out of the two prisoners' reach.

"You can think of this in the days ahead," the crook taunted. "And now—good-by!"

Turning, he ambled up the steps. Nancy heard mocking laughter as the trap door was slammed shut. Soon a deathlike quiet fell on the shack.

"Mr. Aborn!" Nancy called.

There was no answer. Nancy's heart beat wildly. Was the man only in a faint or had something worse happened to him?

Holding her breath, she strained her ears to see if she could detect any sign of life. A few seconds later Nancy caught faint sounds of inhaling and exhaling.

"Thank goodness," she thought.

Presently the man stirred, and regaining consciousness, looked about. Seeing Nancy, he exclaimed, "Now I remember! We were so near freedom."

"Yes, we were, Mr. Aborn. And we may get out of here yet. I'm trying to slip this rope off my wrists. In the meantime, I want to tell you why I didn't mention that Laura is at my home. I was about to do so when you urged that we leave the shack as fast as possible."

"I see and I forgive you," said Mr. Aborn. "Never having met you, Dowd's announcement gave me a momentary feeling of distrust in you. But that's gone now."

"Then would you mind telling me about Laura's mother and the estate she left?" Nancy requested, as she worked to free her hands.

"I'll be glad to. Mrs. Pendleton appointed the Monroe National Bank executor of her estate and me as Laura's guardian. During Mrs. Pendleton's long illness she had all her securities taken from her private safe-deposit box and put in care of the bank. They were turned over to the custodian department and kept in the bank's personal vault."

"Then how could Stumpy Dowd get them?" Nancy asked.

"That's the mystery. He didn't say."

Nancy was convinced now that a good portion of Laura's inheritance must be among the securities stolen from the bank. She asked whether Mrs. Pendleton had left a large estate.

Mr. Aborn nodded. "Laura is a very wealthy young woman," he said, then went on to explain that at the time of Mrs. Pendleton's death, the Aborns were abroad. Upon their arrival in New York, Mrs. Aborn had received word of her mother's illness. It was then that Laura had been asked to postpone coming to Melrose Lake until his wife's return.

"Laura was staying on at her boarding school

with the headmistress until our trip to Melrose."

"She never received your letter," Nancy told him. "The Dowds must have intercepted it. Soon they told her to come."

Just then Nancy thought she had found the trick to freeing her hands, but a moment later she sighed in discouragement. The rope still bound her wrists.

"At least we have a light," she said. Fortunately, Stumpy Dowd had forgotten the lantern.

"Yes, but the oil is burning low," Mr. Aborn remarked quietly. "When it's gone we'll be in the dark—as I have been for the past two weeks."

Nancy shuddered. "Did Stumpy bring you food in little packages?"

"Yes, when he thought of it. He kept me alive just to pump me for information, and threatened to harm Laura if I didn't tell him what he wanted to know."

Suddenly Nancy felt the rope which chafed her wrists slacken. At the same time the light went out. The cellar was plunged into darkness.

CHAPTER XV

Plans for Rescue

BACK in River Heights, meanwhile, Hannah Gruen had spent a restless and worried evening, expecting to hear Nancy's convertible pull into the driveway at any moment. Moreover, Mr. Drew had failed to call at the appointed hour and Hannah had no knowledge of how to contact the lawyer.

At ten thirty, when the front doorbell rang, the housekeeper limped hurriedly to answer it. Instantly she felt a sense of keen disappointment.

"Oh, hello, Laura," she said, and turned to greet Don Cameron. "Did you have a good time at the barbecue?"

"It was wonderful!" Laura exclaimed happily, as she and Don entered the house.

"Certainly was fun," Don agreed. "Too bad Nancy wasn't with us. Where is she, Mrs. Gruen?"

At these words tears welled up in Hannah's eyes. She told of not hearing from either Nancy or Mr. Drew that evening. "I'm so upset," she said. "What will we do? Call the police?"

"Probably Nancy decided to stay overnight at the Beach Cliff Hotel," Laura said at once. "Have you called there to find out?"

"No, because Nancy always calls when she changes her plans."

Don, greatly concerned, went at once to the telephone. Impatiently the young man waited for a response to his ring.

The hotel telephone operator answered. When Don asked for Nancy Drew, the girl said, "Just a moment." It was nearly five minutes before she told him:

"We are unable to reach your party. Miss Drew is not in the hotel."

"Then she didn't check out earlier this evening?" Don inquired.

"No. Miss Drew is still registered."

Don Cameron hung up, a drawn expression on his face. He told the others what he had learned.

"Oh, I just know something has happened to Nancy!" Laura cried, her lower lip quivering with nervousness. "And it's all my fault."

Hannah took the girl into her arms. "You must not feel this way," she said gently. "Nancy is trying to help you because she wants to."

Don spoke up, "I don't know whether we should notify the police or drive to Melrose Lake ourselves."

As the three hesitated, they heard an automobile stop in front of the house. Then a door slammed. Don looked out the window.

"It's a man," he said. "He's coming to the door."

Don opened the door to Carson Drew, who came inside immediately. He greeted Hannah and Don. Then, after being introduced to Laura Pendleton and bidding her welcome to his home, the lawyer asked:

"Where's Nancy? Upstairs?"

When told that his daughter had not returned from her investigation at Melrose Lake, the lawyer was gravely concerned.

"I don't like the sound of this at all," he said. "I had no idea that Nancy was planning to sleuth in Mr. Aborn's home at night."

"She mentioned something about wanting to pay another visit to a mysterious shack in the woods, Mr. Drew," Hannah volunteered. "But I don't know where it's located."

Carson Drew's anxiety deepened. "It would be just like Nancy to follow up a good clue," he said, "particularly if she thinks there is something odd about the shack. She never gives up until she figures out the solution to whatever the problem is."

Despite his worry, Nancy's father uttered these words proudly. He had often admired the initiative his daughter displayed when she was trying to unravel a mystery.

"I think you're on the right track, Mr. Drew," Don Cameron said thoughtfully. "Since Nancy hasn't returned to the hotel, there are three possibilities—she's had car trouble, something has happened to her in the woods—"

"Or the Aborns have discovered Nancy prowling about their house," Laura put in fearfully. "And if that is the case, there's no telling what they may do to her!"

The girl quickly mentioned a few of the things which had happened in her brief stay at the Aborns.

"I'll leave for Melrose Lake immediately," Mr. Drew announced. "If I don't find Nancy in a very short time, I'm going to notify the police that she's missing!"

The others begged Mr. Drew to let them accompany him. The lawyer thought it best for Hannah to remain at home in case Nancy should call.

"But I'll be glad to have you accompany me, Laura and Don," he added.

Don hurried to the telephone to notify his parents of the plan, while Laura went for a coat.

Then they went outside and got into Mr. Drew's car.

"Be sure to call me as soon as you've found out something!" Hannah called.

"Don't worry, we will!"

Nancy's father was a skillful driver and right now he was intent upon reaching the lake as soon as possible. He could barely restrain himself from breaking the speed limits.

"This is one time I wish I had a helicopter," he told the two young people.

"It wouldn't do you much good at Melrose Lake, Mr. Drew," said Laura. "It's a pretty thickly wooded area. I doubt that you'd find a landing strip."

Don realized that this remark, although unintentional, heightened Carson Drew's worry about Nancy being lost in the woods. He changed the subject quickly.

"I thought you weren't due home until Sunday, sir," Don said.

"That's right," the lawyer replied, his eyes intent on the highway ahead. "In Cincinnati late this afternoon I had a call from Chief McGinnis of the River Heights police. He thought it was imperative for me to return home immediately."

Mr. Drew proceeded to tell Don and Laura the complete story of the embezzlement case.

Laura looked worried. "The Monroe National Bank had my mother's securities!" she exclaimed. "You don't suppose—"

"Maybe," Don put in, "Nancy learned something in connection with this at the Aborn house and is staying to get more information."

"Oh, she shouldn't have done it!" Laura cried out fearfully.

"Now there may not be anything to your theory," Mr. Drew remarked. "Don't borrow trouble."

Don patted Laura's shoulder. "Sure. We have enough worries as it is. Mr. Drew, you were telling us why you came back early."

"Yes. Although I'm making a private investigation for Mr. Seward, the bank president, Chief McGinnis has been helping me on an unofficial basis. We're old friends, you see.

"When Nancy told me that two of the suspects —the Dowds—were in the acting profession and had been out of town recently, I had a hunch they might tie in with the case. I asked the chief to check on any past records the couple might have, and call me in Cincinnati."

At this point Carson Drew explained that Chief McGinnis had learned that the Dowds both had records for theft and embezzlement. Each had served prison terms. Using various aliases, they had either acted or worked in theaters in several states and among other crimes had robbed the ticket offices.

"When the chief told me this," said Carson Drew, "I asked him to take the list of missing securities to various brokerage offices in the River Heights area. He did this and found that during the past few days all of them had been sold by a woman."

"The same woman?" Don asked.

"Apparently not," Mr. Drew replied. "At least when Chief McGinnis asked for the woman's description it was different every time."

"How odd!" Laura exclaimed. "Could it have been Mrs. Dowd? Since she's an actress she must be good at disguise."

"You may be right," Mr. Drew acknowledged. "Anyway, the chief sent two officers to their house to pick up the Dowds for questioning."

"Did they find them?" Don asked eagerly.

The lawyer shook his head. "When the police got to the house they learned that the actor and actress had had a man caller earlier in the day and that the three had left together. Mr. Dowd said they would not be back."

"How discouraging for you"—Laura sighed in sympathy—"but I'm sure you'll find them."

"There's a state alarm out for the couple," Mr. Drew said. "They shouldn't be able to get very far."

"What do the Dowds look like?" Laura asked.

In reply, the lawyer took two photographs from his breast pocket and handed them to her.

Laura held the pictures toward the light on the dashboard. She shook her head in disbelief. "These are the Dowds?" she repeated.

"Yes, why? Have you seen them before?"

Laura said in a tense voice, "I know them as Mr. and Mrs. Aborn. Oh, Mr. Drew, if they've caught Nancy, she's in real danger!"

CHAPTER XVI

A Speedy Getaway

UNAWARE that help was coming, Nancy worked feverishly to slip her hands out of the ropes in the dark cellar of the shack.

"How are you doing?" Jacob Aborn asked her.

"The bonds are becoming looser," Nancy replied.

Suddenly she recalled Hannah's promise to send the police to the Aborns' home if she had not returned at a reasonable hour. When she told the imprisoned man about this, it seemed to give him courage.

However, to herself Nancy said, "By that time those criminals will have escaped. They may even prevent Hannah from carrying out her plan! And both Laura and Hannah may be harmed!"

As if to offset this alarming possibility, the ropes around Nancy's hands suddenly pulled free.

"I did it!" she exclaimed, and Mr. Aborn sprang from his bench, crying, "We'll be able to escape!"

Nancy did not respond, for she was working grimly at the ropes which bound her feet. "If I could only see!" she muttered.

Then she remembered the packet of matches in her skirt pocket. She took it out and lighted a match, which she stuck in a crack in the wall. As the light burned she worked to untie the knots that bound her ankles. Several more matches were used before she was free.

"Miss Drew, you're the most ingenious girl I've ever met!" Mr. Aborn said admiringly. "I wish I could think that fast. It just occurred to me that there's a can of kerosene under the stairs. You might fill the lantern."

Nancy found the can and in a few seconds the place was aglow with light.

"Now I'll open the padlock again," Nancy told Mr. Aborn.

After getting the key she hurried to the side of Laura's guardian. A minute later the chains fell to the floor with a loud thud.

"At last!" Jacob Aborn cried in relief.

"Our next step," said Nancy, "is to get out of here as fast as we can and then try to alert the police."

"It's my bet," her companion said, "that Dowd has already skipped town."

Nancy was inclined to agree, but since the swindler had not expected his two prisoners to escape, he might still be at the Aborn house with his wife.

"We'll head for my car," Nancy said, "and decide what we'll do when we reach it."

Jacob Aborn moved forward several steps, then his knees began to tremble. "My legs will be all right after I've used them for a few minutes," he apologized.

But try as he would, the man was unable to climb the stairway unassisted. Nancy reached out a strong arm to help him. At last they reached the top of the stairway.

The young sleuth led the way to the door, unbolted it, and the two stepped outside.

"What a relief!" Jacob Aborn gasped, filling his lungs with pure air.

In the east, the moon had risen over the woods and the sky was peppered with stars. The route among the trees would be easy to find in the clear night. Yet Nancy glanced uneasily at her companion, wondering if he would be able to walk to the car.

As if reading her thoughts, Aborn said, "I'm fine now. Let's go!"

Nancy offered her arm again, and at a slow pace they walked across the clearing and entered the woods. They had gone but a short way when Mr. Aborn sank down on a log, breathing heavily.

"You go on without me, Nancy," he said in a voice shaky with fatigue. "I can't do it."

"Just rest here for a moment," Nancy said encouragingly, unwilling to leave the man.

Shortly, Mr. Aborn felt he could continue. Leaning heavily on Nancy, he moved forward, refusing to pause again even for a brief rest.

"You're a very kind girl to help me," he said hoarsely.

Nancy replied modestly, "I'm *so* glad I found you. Think of what it means to Laura to have her real guardian found! I know she will be happy living with you and your wife."

At the mention of his wife's name Mr. Aborn said he was grateful that she had gone away before the Dowds invaded their home. "She might have been made a prisoner too!" he declared.

Presently, with a feeling of relief, Nancy caught sight of her convertible standing among the bushes where she had left it. After she had helped Mr. Aborn into the front seat, Nancy took her place behind the steering wheel.

"Now we'll drive to the nearest police station," she announced. "You direct me."

She inserted the key and tried the starter. To Nancy's surprise, the motor did not turn over.

"That's funny," she said, and tried again. Nothing happened. Next, Nancy glanced at the fuel gauge. It registered half full.

"I wonder if your battery's dead," Mr. Aborn said in a faint voice.

"I think not," Nancy replied, as she reached into the glove compartment and took out an extra flashlight she kept there for emergencies.

She got out of the car, lifted the hood, and flashed her light inside. She had taken a course in automobile mechanics and knew the possible sources of trouble.

"I see what the trouble is," Nancy called. "The distributor has been uncapped and the rotor's missing! This is sabotage!" Without this necessary part the car could not start. "I'm sure that Mr. Dowd is the saboteur," she added angrily.

Mr. Aborn sighed resignedly. "Stumpy Dowd leaves no stones unturned," he said in a tired voice. "Just in case we might escape he wanted to make certain we'd have no transportation. I'm afraid, Nancy, that we'll have to go to the main highway for help."

As Mr. Aborn spoke, Nancy heard a car motor not far away. Eagerly she looked to right and left but saw no approaching headlights.

"Quick! Duck down!" Mr. Aborn whispered, and Nancy crouched in the bushes alongside her car.

A dark foreign sports car emerged from the Eagle Rock lane, then made a left-hand turn in the direction of Twin Lakes!

"It's the Dowds making a getaway!" Mr. Aborn said. "We're too late!"

Nancy was alarmed by this turn of events. She wondered why Stumpy Dowd was not heading toward River Heights. Had he given up the idea of going to the Drews' residence and forcing Laura Pendleton to give him the jewels? Or was he taking an alternative route there?

"Oh dear! I wish there were a telephone nearby!" Nancy moaned. She told Mr. Aborn that his had been disconnected.

Jacob Aborn spoke up. "Nancy, I'm sure that Dowd and his wife have left my house for good. I think the best plan is for us to go there."

"Yes," Nancy agreed. "After you're safely inside I'll go for help."

"I can't let you do that," Jacob Aborn protested. "Few cars come along this road at night. You'll have an extremely long walk before you reach the main highway."

Silently Nancy agreed, but she also noted that the man's strength was almost spent. She helped him from the car, and the two slowly approached the lane that led to Mr. Aborn's house.

"Oh, if I could only get my hands on that scoundrel!" the man muttered.

The thought gave him new strength, and he moved forward again. Cautiously the two crept toward the house, approaching it from the rear.

"We'd better make certain that no one's here," Nancy whispered.

As they drew near the back door she saw that it stood ajar, as though someone had left hurriedly without taking time to shut it.

With Jacob Aborn close behind her, Nancy stepped cautiously into the kitchen. There was profound silence. The place appeared deserted.

Crossing the room on tiptoe, Nancy and Mr. Aborn walked toward the living room. He clicked on a light. Everything was in disorder. A chair had been overturned and papers were scattered about.

"The Dowds certainly made a thorough search," Nancy remarked.

Just then Mr. Aborn's eyes fell upon the wall safe which stood open. With a cry of alarm he tottered across the room to look inside. Everything had been taken out.

Mr. Aborn groaned. He told Nancy that a sizable sum of his own money had been in the safe, along with shares of negotiable stock. Stumpy Dowd had forced him to tell the safe's combination on threat of harming Laura.

Mr. Aborn, white as starch, sank into a nearby chair and buried his head in his hands. "Nearly all my securities were in there," he said. One quick glance at him told Nancy that the man was on the verge of a complete collapse. She could not leave him alone, yet how could she get help without doing so?

A second later she and Mr. Aborn were startled to hear a car driving up the lane. Were the Dowds returning? Had the couple merely gone out for a while, or had they forgotten something in their hasty flight?

Nancy's next thought was far worse than either of these. Had Stumpy Dowd somehow learned that his two prisoners had escaped?

CHAPTER XVII

Two-way Detecting

As THE automobile pulled to a halt, Mr. Aborn slumped to the floor in a faint. Evidently he had shared Nancy's thought that the Dowds were returning, and would force their way in. The terrifying thought that he might become a prisoner again had been too much for the exhausted man.

"Oh!" Nancy cried out.

From the window Nancy saw four people hurriedly alighting from the car. A moment later the bell rang and a woman's voice cried, "Mr. Aborn —Mr. Aborn—please let us in. It's the Donnells!"

Nancy hurried to the front door and flung it open. "Cathy! Jim!" she cried out. "Oh, you don't know how glad I am to see you!"

The two young people introduced Nancy to their parents, a good-looking couple in their forties. Then they stepped inside.

"What are you doing here, Nancy?" Jim Donnell asked, puzzled at the girl's disheveled appearance. "What's going on?"

Nancy replied by saying Mr. Aborn was ill, and there was no time for further explanation right now. She hastily led the family into the living room. When they saw their unconscious friend on the floor, Mrs. Donnell rushed forward with an excited cry.

"How dreadful!" she exclaimed.

As she knelt down, the kindly woman said she was a registered nurse. After a brief examination of the patient she reported that Mr. Aborn appeared to be suffering from malnutrition and shock.

While Jim and his father lifted him onto the couch, Nancy told what had happened to him. The Donnells were stunned.

Before they could discuss it, however, Nancy turned to Jim. "Two phone calls must be made right away," she said. "Would you be able to take care of them for me?"

"Glad to," the boy said. "I suppose you want me to notify the police to pick up Stumpy Dowd—"

"Yes," Nancy said tersely, and described the black foreign car.

She next asked Jim to call Chief McGinnis at River Heights and tell him to have extra men patrol the Drew home. "Find out if Mrs. Gruen and

Laura are all right," she requested, "and see if our housekeeper knows where to get in touch with Dad."

Jim said he would do all of these things. As soon as he returned, he would try to fix Nancy's car.

After Jim left, Nancy turned to the others. Mr. Aborn had regained consciousness and said he felt better and able to talk.

"Lillian," he said, giving Mrs. Donnell a wan smile, "the angels must have sent you. How did you know we were in trouble here?"

"We didn't for sure," Mr. Donnell replied gravely, "until tonight—it's a long story."

The gray-haired man said that he and his wife had been amazed to hear on Tuesday from their children that Marian Aborn had returned from Florida and that she and Jacob had met Laura Pendleton at Twin Lakes.

"We were sure you would have told us of your change of plans, if this were true, Jacob," he said to his old friend. "Anyway, we came over here yesterday morning to say hello and meet Laura. No one answered the bell."

"We concluded," said Mrs. Donnell, "that Nancy Drew had been mistaken in thinking that you were coming back here—anyway, we remembered you saying that due to the illness of Marian's mother you would not be able to come here with Laura until after your wife's return."

"That's right," said Mr. Aborn. He explained to Nancy that first there had been legal technicalities regarding his appointment as the orphan's guardian, since he had been living in another state. That was why his ward had remained at her boarding school.

Mrs. Donnell went on to say that this evening they had received a telephone call from Mrs. Aborn who was still in Florida. "Marian had tried several times to get you and was upset to learn that the phone here was disconnected. She called us to see why."

"My wife hadn't heard from me in over two weeks," Mr. Aborn stated.

Mrs. Donnell said, "But Marian thought she had. Mrs. Aborn sent telegrams here and replies came to her in Florida."

Mr. Donnell said that when the family heard that Marian Aborn was indeed in Florida, they were fearful something was terribly wrong.

"We told Marian what we knew, suggested she come home immediately, and said we would come over here right away to see what we could uncover."

"Thank goodness you did," Nancy sighed, and Mr. Aborn gave his friends a grateful smile. Then he asked, "How is Marian's mother?"

"Getting along very well."

"When will my wife arrive?" Mr. Aborn asked anxiously.

"She's taking a night plane from Miami to the Hamilton airport," Mrs. Donnell replied. "My husband will meet her."

Cathy's mother then went to the kitchen to prepare a light meal for Mr. Aborn. Nancy excused herself and went to wash her face, legs, and grimy hands. Refreshed, she returned to the living room, wondering what was keeping Jim so long.

"He'll be here soon, Nancy," said Cathy.

"I'll feel much better when I know everything's all right at home," Nancy replied.

While Mr. Aborn ate, the pretty detective told the others of Stumpy Dowd's connection with Mr. Drew's case.

"What a story!" Mr. Donnell exclaimed.

Nancy excused herself for a moment and went to the front door to listen for Jim's car. As she stood on the steps her heart suddenly leaped. A tall figure stood up from behind a bush near the front steps.

"Nancy?" a man's voice called softly.

Nancy knew who it was. "Dad!" she cried out.

Carson Drew leaped the steps and gave his daughter a resounding kiss. "Are you all right?" he whispered.

When Nancy said yes, and that it was safe to

talk aloud, Don Cameron and Laura emerged from some shrubbery.

"We saw lights and heard voices," Laura explained. "We thought it was the Aborns. What's going on here, Nancy?"

"Yes, tell us!" Don urged.

Once again Nancy explained what had happened. Carson Drew listened to his daughter's story of her encounter with the thief, a stern expression on his face.

"You were lucky to come out of this so well," he remarked.

"Yes," Laura agreed. "And it's so wonderful to have a guardian whom you say is nice!"

"Mr. Aborn is a fine person, Laura," Nancy said. "I'll take you in to meet him in a minute."

Carson Drew now brought Nancy up to date on his news, and ended by saying, "We were so worried we drove here immediately, not even taking time to call the police."

Don added that they had left Mr. Drew's car at the end of the lane and were scouting the house to see if Nancy were inside when she had appeared on the front steps.

"How many times I wished you were here!" said Nancy. She now suggested that everyone come into the house to meet the others. "Jim Donnell," she added, "should return any minute."

"I'll wait for the young man out here and act

as guard in case the Dowds show up," Carson Drew said, sitting down on a step. "The rest of you run along—"

As Nancy walked inside with Don and Laura she saw that Mr. and Mrs. Donnell were helping Mr. Aborn up the stairs to his bedroom. Hearing voices, the guardian turned, looked at his ward, and exclaimed:

"Laura dear—at last—I'd know you anywhere! You look just like your mother!"

"Mr. Aborn!" Laura cried out. She raced up the steps and gave her guardian a big kiss.

Introductions were quickly made, and when Mr. Aborn was settled in his bed, he had a visit with Laura and Nancy. But after they had chatted for a few minutes the girls could see that the man needed sleep badly.

"We'll say good night now," said Nancy. "Sweet dreams." She turned off the light, and they went downstairs.

When Nancy and Laura reached the first floor, they found Mr. Drew and Jim Donnell talking in the hall with a state trooper. While Cathy took Laura aside, Nancy walked toward the group.

She was introduced to Sergeant Murphy, then Carson Drew explained to her that the state police were putting all available cars on the chase and hoped to round up the Dowds and their accomplice shortly.

"Good!" Nancy exclaimed. "But what about Mrs. Gruen?"

Sergeant Murphy said that he had talked with Chief McGinnis. The River Heights official had immediately sent a patrol car and four men to the Drews' home.

"Your housekeeper was relieved to hear that you, Miss Drew, had been found," he reported. "Nothing unusual has happened at your home tonight. But it will be closely guarded until the Dowds and their accomplice are caught."

"Oh, I'm glad," said Nancy. Sergeant Murphy left, after saying he would check back later.

Nancy and Mr. Drew walked into the living room, and she introduced her father to Mr. and Mrs. Donnell and Cathy. After a few minutes of excited conversation, the young sleuth said:

"Dad, I have a hunch that the man 'Fred' whom Stumpy Dowd mentioned is someone employed at the Monroe National Bank. Tell me, was Mrs. Pendleton's name ever mentioned in connection with the missing securities?"

Mr. Drew shook his head. "No, Nancy, it wasn't."

"Then," said Nancy, "I think we're going to find that Laura's bonds were never deposited in the bank's vault. Whoever took them and passed them on to Stumpy Dowd must be someone who works in the custodian department of the bank."

"That's good reasoning, Nancy," her father agreed, "but we have checked almost all the employees and they've been given a clean bill of health. One man, Mr. Hamilton's assistant, has been on vacation and we won't be able to interview him for another week or so."

"What's the man's name?" Nancy asked.

Mr. Drew consulted a list of names which he took from his pocket. "William Frednich."

Nancy snapped her fingers. "Frednich! Maybe *he's* the 'Fred' the Dowds were talking about. And if he is," she continued excitedly, "I think they're together and I believe I know where the Dowds are hiding out with this man!"

Carson Drew looked at his daughter in amazement. "Where?" he asked.

"Not far from here," Nancy said mysteriously. Then she jumped up from her chair. "Let's find out, Dad!"

CHAPTER XVIII

Night Trail

CARSON DREW, startled, looked at his daughter.

"Where do you think the Dowds and Fred are hiding, Nancy?"

"In a bungalow on Twin Lakes—the one I told you we stayed in after Laura rescued us," she explained. "My main reasons for thinking so are these: I saw a black foreign car come from there, and the place was well-stocked with food. Fred may have been living there."

"Go on. This is interesting," the lawyer said.

Nancy's hunch was that the thieves had first planned the bank theft, then the Dowds had rented the bungalow under an assumed name.

"Makes sense." Carson Drew nodded.

"Fred," Nancy continued, "knew of Laura's large estate and jewelry, and got the idea of having Stumpy Dowd impersonate Mr. Aborn. In order to get the jewelry they had to have Laura with them, so they decided to take her to the Melrose Lake house."

"Good logic," said Mr. Drew. "Then, when the real Mr. Aborn appeared, they had to kidnap him temporarily. Well, we'll follow your hunch. Shall we go?"

The others offered to go, but Mr. Drew thought that the Donnells should stay with Mr. Aborn and Laura.

"Please do," Nancy added. "After all, my hunch could be wrong. The Dowds may return here."

"We'll nab 'em if they do!" Jim said determinedly.

A few minutes later Mr. Drew's car was on the detour again, heading for the Twin Lakes road. When they reached it, there were no other cars in evidence.

"That's odd," said Nancy, knowing that this was the only road which connected the two resorts.

"Oh, oh!" said Don. "Look!"

Mr. Drew had also seen a small red light a few hundred feet distant. He slowed up. Ahead was a gate obstruction across the highway. On it was nailed a sign which read:

ROAD UNDER CONSTRUCTION
Travel at your own risk

"This is great!" Mr. Drew remarked unhappily.

"Maybe it won't be too bad," Nancy said. "I came this way the other day and I think I know all the turns."

"Why don't we try it, sir?" Don spoke up.

"All right."

Don got out of the car and moved the barrier enough so Mr. Drew could drive through. They went slowly, because of the steam shovels, bulldozers, and equipment parked along the road.

To make matters worse, the pavement was gone in places where repairs were being made. The car tires wallowed in soft dirt.

Soon, however, they reached the end of the construction section and Carson Drew stepped on the accelerator. The car responded with a burst of speed.

"We're not far from Twin Lakes now," Nancy said as she spotted a few familiar landmarks.

Don wanted to know what the plan would be when they reached the bungalow. Mr. Drew said they would first check to see if the foreign car were in the vicinity. "Of course it will be hidden."

"Next," Nancy added, "we'll have to make sure Fred and the Dowds are there, and not some innocent people. But if Stumpy's there, we'll notify the police. Right, Dad?"

"Unless Dowd sees us first," he said grimly.

Nancy said she hoped this would not happen.

"But I suppose they probably will have someone acting as a lookout."

"As I understand it, Nancy," said her father, "the bungalow is in an isolated spot."

"Yes, and there are a lot of trees around it."

"Could anyone inside the house make a getaway by boat?" Don asked.

"Not easily," Nancy answered. "The bungalow is not built over the water. It's some distance from the lake and there's no dock where a boat could be tied." Presently she said, "We're about a mile from the bungalow."

Carson Drew's face tensed. He drove to a point about a tenth of a mile from the lane leading down to the bungalow, then stopped the car in a clearing off the road.

"We'll cover the rest of the distance on foot," he announced.

As Nancy got out the right-hand side of the car after Don she glanced at the luminous dial on the clock. It was three o'clock in the morning!

Walking three abreast, the sleuths saw the bungalow below. It was in darkness.

"I don't see any sign of a car," Don whispered to Nancy, as he guided her by the arm.

Carson Drew was silent, but suddenly he jerked to attention. A twig had snapped. Now they saw a man walking toward the trio through the woods!

As Don, Nancy, and Mr. Drew ducked behind

some shrubbery, they noticed that the man approaching them was carrying a fishing pole and a box of the type ordinarily used for bait.

Passing by the watchers, he walked unhurriedly toward the beach. At this moment the moon chose to show itself brilliantly, and Nancy observed that the man was tall and heavy.

"Hello, Sam," he said, and now the watchers could see a rowboat and passenger gliding out of the shadows.

"I hope the fish are biting well this morning." His voice carried clearly in the stillness.

The fisherman deposited his gear in the boat, and the two companions shoved off. They were barely out of sight when Don whispered hoarsely, "A light in the bungalow."

From the second-story window had come a flash of light. It did not reappear.

"Someone's up there!" Nancy whispered. "Maybe the fisherman alerted him."

"Let's circle the house," said Carson Drew, and suggested that he take the left half of the circle while Nancy and Don took the right. They would meet back at this same spot in a few minutes.

"Be careful now," he warned the young people.

"You too, Dad," Nancy said.

The route Nancy and Don took led past the door into the first floor of the boathouse bungalow. Cautiously they listened at the exit. There was no sound from within. They went on to the beach side.

The two tiptoed among the shadows as far as the center of the rear of the building without incident, then quietly returned to the meeting place. When they arrived, Mr. Drew was not there.

"That's funny," said Nancy, a little alarmed. "Where *is* Dad?"

Just then she and Don heard a low groan. It seemed to come from behind a tree about twenty feet away. Forgetting caution, the couple rushed to the spot. Behind its broad trunk a man lay sprawled on the ground. Mr. Drew!

"Dad!" Nancy exclaimed, kneeling down. She felt the lawyer's pulse. It was steady.

"I think he was knocked out," said Don angrily. "Nancy, you're right about this being a hide-out. We must get the police!"

"And right away!" Nancy agreed, as Carson Drew sat up groggily. In a moment he could talk.

The lawyer said that after leaving Nancy and Don he had started around the bungalow. Someone had come from behind and struck him. "I suppose he dragged me here."

"Stumpy Dowd, I'll bet!" Nancy exclaimed. "And this may mean that he and his wife made a getaway while Don and I were on the other side of the bungalow! Dad, do you feel well enough to try to follow them?"

"Yes, but where did they go?" he asked. "And how? By boat, car, or on foot?"

As if in answer to his question, the three suddenly saw in the clear moonlight the figures of two men and a woman running up the bungalow lane toward the road. Each man carried a big suitcase. Laura's inheritance and Mr. Aborn's little fortune!

"After them!" Don cried.

But Mr. Drew could not make it. He tottered unsteadily and leaned against the pine. "Go on!" he said.

"No!" Nancy replied quickly. "Don, bring Dad's car here, will you?"

As the boy started off, the trio heard the muffled backfire of an automobile coming from the direction of the woods across the main road.

"Hurry, Don!" Nancy urged. "They had a car hidden there."

By the time Don returned, Carson Drew felt better. He suggested that Nancy drive, since she was more familiar with the road. When everyone was in the car, with the lawyer in the rear seat, they took off.

Upon reaching the road, the young sleuth turned right. "I think this is the direction the other car took," she said. "Anyway, it leads to Stamford, where I know there's a state police headquarters."

Carson Drew sat up groggily

The road became rough and was full of sharp turns. Nancy drove fast but carefully, slowing at each curve. There was no sign of another car until Don suddenly cried out:

"I think we're approaching a car!"

Nancy peered forward intently. She saw nothing but the road ahead.

"It's hidden now by that hill in front of us," Don told her.

There was a long moment of suspense, then Nancy exclaimed, "I see it!"

"Do you think it's the Dowds?" Don asked.

"It could be," Mr. Drew replied.

As the car reached a smooth, straight piece of road, Nancy put it to a faster and faster pace.

"We're gaining on them!" Don said exuberantly.

Little by little the Drew sedan crept up on the car ahead. Soon its headlights spotlighted the rear of the other vehicle—a black foreign car! Three figures were silhouetted inside it!

At the same moment Nancy caught sight of a huge black-and-white checkerboard sign at the side of the road. A bad curve ahead! With well-timed precision, Nancy eased up on her speed and gradually used her brake, knowing that abrupt pressure might cause a bad skid.

"That other driver isn't paying any attention to the warning!" Don exclaimed.

The snakelike curve was only a few hundred feet ahead on a steep downgrade. The occupants of the Drew sedan held their breath. Would the others make the turn? There came a violent screech of brakes.

"Oh no!" Nancy cried out in horror.

As she and her companions watched, the foreign car shot off the edge of the road and plunged down a steep cliff!

CHAPTER XIX

Missing Property

STUNNED by the accident to the speeding car, Nancy brought the sedan to a halt at the curve. Everyone inside was reluctant to look down into the ravine below, from which there was not a sound.

But only for an instant. Then Carson Drew urged, "Out, everyone, quickly! We must do what we can for those people!"

Nancy and Don sprang from the car and rushed to the edge of the road. The lawyer was close behind them.

As the three gazed down into the ravine, the first light of dawn revealed that the foreign car had rolled nearly to the bottom of it and overturned against a boulder. A wheel had been torn loose from its axle and the body had been smashed in. There was no sign of any of the three occupants.

A silence held the trio above. It was inconceivable that anyone in the wreck could be alive!

At last Carson Drew found his voice. "I guess we'd better notify the police and emergency squad," he said.

Don agreed, but Nancy thought they should first see if by chance any of the accident victims were alive.

Mr. Drew and Don nodded, and followed Nancy as she scrambled down the incline. Nancy, in the lead, gasped as she saw the body of a strange man, apparently not the driver, which had been flung out of the car into a clump of bushes near the wreck. She also noticed gasoline spilling from a hole in the tank. Vaguely she thought of fire and an explosion.

"Hurry!" she urged.

As the three drew closer they saw a man's leg and a woman's high-heeled shoe protruding from beneath the left-hand side of the car.

With frantic haste Don and Mr. Drew dragged the man out, while Nancy tugged at the woman's body. Stumpy Dowd and his wife! Both were breathing, but unconscious. The victims, cut and badly bruised, were carried to a safe place on the grass.

"Now let's see about the other man, Mr. Drew," urged Don.

As they headed for the bushes where he lay,

Nancy stared at the car. "The suitcases!" she thought. "Laura's inheritance and Mr. Aborn's little fortune! I must get them out before they may be burned up!"

Crawling under the wreck, she began to grope about frantically. Her hand struck a suitcase and she dragged it out.

At that instant Nancy realized how hot the metal was. There might be spontaneous combustion at any second. She must work fast to save the second suitcase!

"It's the only way I can ever repay Laura for saving my life on Twin Lakes!" Nancy thought.

By feeling around she found the bag and triumphantly brought it out, only to be jerked from the scene by Carson Drew and Don.

"Nancy!" Carson Drew cried, white-faced and horror-stricken. "Are you mad? Those suitcases aren't worth your life!"

There was a sudden explosion. Then flames enveloped the car and the dry grass in the immediate vicinity began to burn.

Don Cameron shuddered, but looked at Nancy, admiration showing in his eyes. "You're the most courageous girl I've ever met," he said slowly. "Nancy, you might have been killed!"

As she herself realized what a narrow escape she had had, Nancy breathed a prayer of thanksgiving.

She was shaken and silent as the men threw dirt on the flames to keep them from spreading. When they finished, Don told Nancy that he and Mr. Drew thought the third man would be all right, although the stranger as well as the Dowds were injured, perhaps seriously.

"Now I suppose we must get the three of them to a hospital as fast as we can," he said.

At that moment they all heard the low whine of an ambulance alarm. This was followed by a police siren.

Nancy, Mr. Drew, and Don looked at one another hopefully. "Do you suppose—" Nancy began.

She was right. Help had come! A moment later police and emergency squad cars stopped at the top of the ravine. Four officers, two stretcher-bearers, and an intern, clad in white, hurried down to the group.

"Thank goodness," said Mr. Drew. Introductions were quickly made, then he asked, "How did you know about the accident?"

An officer, Lieutenant Gill, told him that a farmer living not far away had seen the speeding car go off the road and notified headquarters.

"When we heard it was a black foreign car, we were suspicious immediately," he said. "Can you identify these people as the Dowds?"

"From pictures, yes," said Mr. Drew, and briefly told the whole story of the Dowd affair up to the present moment.

"And I can testify that they were impersonating the Aborns," Nancy added.

"Anybody know who the other man is?" Lieutenant Gill inquired.

"I believe," Mr. Drew replied, "that he's William Frednich, assistant to the president of the River Heights branch of the Monroe National Bank. He's suspected of removing certain securities from the bank."

During this conversation the intern had been examining the accident victims and the attendants had laid them on stretchers. The doctor reported that the victims had been given first aid and had revived. They would be in good shape after a short stay in the hospital.

"They'll get a nice long rest after that," said Lieutenant Gill, "in the state pen. I shan't try to question them now."

As the prisoners were carried up to the ambulance, with the others following, Lieutenant Gill explained to the Dowds how Nancy had saved them from being burned in the wreckage.

"I don't believe it," said Stumpy ungratefully.

His wife was more gracious. "Thanks, Miss Drew. And I want to tell you I'm tired of this whole business. You're only a kid but you've really taught me a lesson."

Nancy did not answer. She found herself choking up, and tears came into her eyes.

As the ambulance moved away, Nancy, quickly brushing her moist eyes dry with the backs of her hands, turned toward the east. She observed that a beautiful sunrise was beginning to flood the sky with brilliant color.

Don yawned. "What do you say we head for home?" he suggested. "Otherwise, I'll never be able to make my sister's wedding this evening."

"Oh dear!" Nancy exclaimed. "I forgot all about it. Please forgive us for keeping you up all night."

Don grinned. "I wouldn't have missed this excitement for anything!"

"I suggest," said Mr. Drew, "that we go back to Nancy's hotel and the Drews will get some sleep. Don, you take my car and return to River Heights. Later, Nancy and I will take a taxi and pick up her convertible at the Aborns'."

"Thank you, sir. I'll do that."

While the three had been talking, Lieutenant Gill had been wedging open one of the two locked suitcases which Nancy had taken from the wrecked car. Mr. Drew and the others walked over as he lifted the lid.

The bag was jammed with feminine clothing. There were several dresses, a large make-up kit, pieces of lingerie, shoes, and several wigs—a gray one, a black hairpiece, and one which was decidedly auburn.

"That clinches it, Dad!" Nancy exclaimed. "Mrs. Dowd must have gone around in disguise to cash the bonds."

"But where's the money she got?" Don asked.

"It must be in the other bag," Nancy suggested, "together with securities and money belonging to Laura Pendleton, Mr. Aborn, and River Heights bank clients."

Lieutenant Gill opened the second suitcase. It contained men's clothing and toilet articles.

"Nancy, you risked your life for this!" Don exclaimed.

Nancy Drew could not believe her eyes. Had she been mistaken in believing that Stumpy Dowd had put the contents of Mr. Aborn's safe in the bags? Quickly she glanced down at the foreign car. Had Laura's inheritance and other people's money burned in it?

The thought stunned the young sleuth. But in a moment an idea came to her.

"There's just a possibility the papers *are* here," she said.

All eyes turned on the girl detective, as the group awaited a further explanation.

CHAPTER XX

A Surprise Gift

"I'M SURE," said Nancy, "that Mr. Dowd not only put the money and securities in one of these suitcases, but never removed them!"

"Then *where* are they?" Don asked.

Nancy smiled. "These bags may have false bottoms!"

Lieutenant Gill said, "Why, of course. I should have thought of that."

Kneeling down, he soon found that Nancy was right. The bottom of each bag opened up, disclosing packages of thousand-dollar bills and securities.

"Good thinking, Nancy," said Don admiringly. "You're a whiz of a detective, all right."

It took Mr. Drew and the officers several minutes to count the large sum of money and make a rough estimate of the value of the stocks and bonds. When they finished, the officer gave Carson Drew a receipt to turn over to the president of the Monroe National Bank. Meanwhile, he would take the stolen property to police headquarters and send on a detailed report.

A few minutes later Nancy's group said good-by to the officers, and returned to Mr. Drew's car. When they reached the Beach Cliff Hotel, Nancy and Mr. Drew got out. They thanked Don for all he had done.

"Don't mention it." The young man grinned. Turning to Nancy, he added, "I kept my date with you yesterday after all!"

As he got into the driver's seat Don said that when he returned the car to the Drews' home he would tell Hannah Gruen what had happened.

It was now very light. Nancy and her father, exhausted, could hardly wait to get a few hours sleep. They tumbled into their beds and slept until noon, then met in the hotel dining room for a hearty brunch.

"How's your head, Dad?" Nancy asked.

"Sound as ever!" Carson Drew said, grinning. "I don't even have a bump."

"Then we have a date," Nancy told him, waving a note. "This was at the desk. I picked it up. The clerk said Jim Donnell left it a little while ago."

"The date's with him?" Mr. Drew asked.

"No. Laura Pendleton. She says she and the

Aborns are thrilled by the news which the police relayed and would like us to come to their house as soon as possible. What do you say, Dad?"

"We'll go."

As Nancy finished her pancakes and sausages she remarked that she could hardly wait to start for the Aborns' home. "I wonder if the Dowds have confessed everything and what Mr. Frednich had to say."

"In my opinion it's an open and shut case," the lawyer replied.

While Mr. Drew paid the hotel bill, Nancy called a taxi and soon the Drews were heading for Eagle Rock Lane. Reaching it, they got out of the cab and the lawyer paid the driver.

Nancy slid in behind the steering wheel of her convertible, as Mr. Drew got in on the other side. The motor started at once. "Good old Jim," Nancy said with a smile, and drove up the lane to the Aborn home.

As she parked, the front door was opened by a woman of about forty-five. Her pretty face showed humor, kindness, and intelligence.

After the Drews had introduced themselves, the woman said she was Marian Aborn and had reached home "in the wee small hours" because her plane was late. "I've been most eager to meet you two," she added, smiling. "How can I ever thank you for all you've done?"

As the callers went inside, Laura Pendleton hurried down from the second floor. After greeting Mr. Drew she gave Nancy a kiss and exclaimed, "Everything is so wonderful—you've captured the thieves and recovered all the money—and I have the nicest guardians anyone could ever hope for!"

"And Jacob and I have a daughter to love!" said Marian Aborn, smiling fondly at Laura.

Nancy asked how Mr. Aborn felt. His wife said, "Come see for yourselves," and led the way to a small study at the rear of the house.

She knocked, then opened the door, and Nancy heard the steady drum of typewriter keys. Jacob Aborn was seated behind the machine.

The erstwhile cellar prisoner already looked like a new man. His face was flooded with color, and his eyes were alert and happy. Now he stood up, greeted the Drews, and expressed his great appreciation for all they had done in recovering his and Laura's property.

He grinned at Nancy. "First time a girl ever risked her life for me!" he said. "To show my appreciation I'm writing my adventure. You know, writing is my business. If I sell this one to a magazine, I'm going to give the proceeds to Nancy's favorite charity—the River Heights Youth Center!"

"Why, that's terrific!" Nancy exclaimed.

Mrs. Aborn's face sobered. She said that she

had not yet heard the entire story of what had happened. Before anyone had a chance to tell her, the doorbell rang. Lieutenant Gill walked in with Chief McGinnis of River Heights and another man. While Nancy greeted the officers, her father hurried to shake hands with the stranger.

"This is Mr. Seward, president of the Monroe National Bank," he announced a moment later, and introduced the dignified white-haired man.

The president's glance included the policemen as he said, "I want to thank all of you in person for the splendid job you did in capturing the Dowds and the two bank employees involved in the thefts."

"There is a fourth man?" Nancy asked in amazement.

Mr. Seward explained that Alma Dowd's brother, Joe Jackson, had been employed by the Monroe National Bank in their vault department for some time. He and Frednich had cooked up the scheme of taking the securities. They had done this between audits of the bank's holdings. Frednich, in his job as assistant custodian, had known exactly how to place his hands on the valuable stocks and bonds.

"Frednich overheard Mrs. Pendleton's discussion with me about Laura and the large estate she would inherit some day," Mr. Seward said, "and also that Mr. Aborn would be her guardian.

When Frednich learned that Laura Pendleton had a valuable jewelry collection, he instantly thought of a swindle scheme. Frednich had chanced to meet Mr. Aborn one time while vacationing at Melrose Lake. He had been amazed by the strong resemblance between Aborn and Stumpy Dowd, whom Alma's brother had introduced to Frednich. He asked Dowd to impersonate Mr. Aborn and to move up the date when Laura would come to the guardian's home. He even deposited some securities with the bank in Stumpy's name, so there would be no question of Dowd's having anything to do with the thefts."

"Where is Joe Jackson now?" Nancy asked.

Chief McGinnis said he would answer this question. "We caught him cruising by the Drews' home. When we stopped the car, he tried to escape. After the whole story broke, we got a confession from him. He was going to burglarize your home, Nancy, to find the jewels."

"There's one thing I don't understand," said Mrs. Aborn. "Why did the Dowds rent the bungalow when they had helped themselves to this house?"

Nancy grinned. "I'm sure I know," she said. "Dowd was smart enough not to want either Frednich or Jackson to stay here—just in case anyone from the bank traced the thefts to them before Dowd could make a getaway. So he had Alma

Dowd rent the bungalow and convinced Frednich that it was a good hide-out."

After Mr. Aborn and Laura had signed statements for the police, the officers and Mr. Seward left. Nancy suddenly felt a sense of loneliness and realized it was because her work on the case was at an end. Would another mystery come her way to solve? she wondered. And it did. In less than a week, Nancy was facing up to the challenge of *The Mystery at Lilac Inn.*

Nancy and her father now said good-by to the family at Eagle Rock. As Nancy gave Laura a farewell hug, she asked, "When will you come to get your jewelry?"

Laura consulted her guardian, who said the next day would be convenient for them to drive to River Heights. "Will three o'clock be all right?"

"Yes indeed."

The following afternoon Laura Pendleton and the Aborns arrived promptly. After iced tea and some of Hannah's delicious open-faced sandwiches, Laura whispered to Mr. Drew that she would love to get her jewelry from the safe. Excusing himself, Nancy's father left the room and returned in a few minutes with the package, which he handed to Laura.

Nancy, meanwhile, was listening to Jacob Aborn's surprising news that he had finished his story and was sending it to a leading magazine.

"Wonderful!" said Nancy. As she said this, she looked up to see Laura standing before her. In the girl's hand was the beautiful aquamarine ring Nancy had admired earlier in the week.

"I'd like you to wear this," Laura said shyly, "as a reminder that our friendship began on the water." Quickly she slipped the ring on the third finger of Nancy's right hand.

The pretty detective gave an exclamation of delight and admired the gift for a long moment. Then she showed it to the others. At last she turned to Laura and said with genuine sincerity:

"The ring is priceless and I'll always treasure it as a reminder of you—although no one can place a value on a true friendship like ours."

Seeing tears in Laura's eyes, Nancy added quickly with a grin, "Even if we had to be shipwrecked to get an introduction!"